THE EDUCATIONAL CONTRACT

The Educational Contract

ISBN 978-1483969756

Cover art by Juanita Rasmus
Cover design by custom-book-tique.com

www.anthropologi.net

THE

EDUCATIONAL

CONTRACT

DR. SHARON WASHINGTON

Anthropologi Publishing

For Mama, Honey, Milah,
and Dennis—my inspiration

ACKNOWLEDGEMENTS

A "Thank You" to Teachers Everywhere

I recently received this note on Facebook from a young man that I taught when he was in seventh and eighth grade. That was about fifteen years ago at a school that five colleagues and I co-founded in New York City. It is a beautiful tribute to "teachers" everywhere–those of you who have a "calling" to teach. Whether you have personally received a note like this one or not, know that what you do has this kind of impact on the very life of children:

"Hey Sharon I was in communion class yesterday and I shared a story that has always been close to my heart. I told the group when I was in junior high I was having a lot of family problems and it started to affect my school work and my behavior, but I had a teacher that never gave up on me. I told them how you fasted and prayed to God that I would change my life. I even started to tear up and so did many people in the group. God listened to you even though it didn't seem like it at the time. I just want to thank you for inspiring me to become a better person and caring so much. You're 1 in a billion. Hopefully God gives me the chance to change someone's life like you did for me. I started working for a nonprofit anti-gang program, I see young kids in the same situation I was in, so if I can change only one kid then I've given back to my community and to people like you. There's nobody that has had such a profound impact on my life like you have. love always Rene"

Table of Contents

THE PREFACE

How we're introduced to the world has everything to do with how we learn. My introduction to the world was quite dramatic. When my mother was pregnant with me, she was diagnosed with cancer in her uterus. The doctors gave her a year to live, if she would abort the baby. The story goes that my mother said: "If I only get a year, what's the point? Besides I asked God for this baby." So they sent her home to die. She asked her pastor to come and pray for her. Two weeks later, the doctors called it remission. She called it a miracle. Nevertheless, when I was born, I was born dead. The doctors, I'm told, worked on getting me to breathe for twenty minutes. Finally, one doctor said to my mom: "Mother, we tried everything we could, but we could not get your baby girl to breathe. Even if we could, she would be brain dead at this point." My mother responded with: "Well. Whatever God wills." And suddenly, I started crying. This is how I was introduced to the world.

Consequently, my mother thought I had something special here to do in this world; so she and my father made me believe that I could do anything. The first five years of my life, I was so indulged by their beliefs that I developed a strong determination to achieve whatever I decided I wanted to do. If I could imagine it, I did it. This belief shaped my confidence. I've always been a very confident learner–understanding new concepts with speed and ease.

My mother further introduced me to the world through books. She read to me incessantly. Reading to children prepares them for the way classroom learning works. It teaches them to listen, absorb information, then, on cue, to respond. It also teaches them language– words, grammar, meaning, the standard language (in this case, standard English). Reading to me set me up to earn mostly A's as a student throughout my school years, although I only went to school about three days a week from third to twelfth grade. I hated school. I had a ritual I carried out two or three times a week on school days: I would wake up, dread the idea of going to school, and I would pray (actually pray to God) that my mom would let me stay home from school that day. Then I would go into my mother's bedroom and say: "Mama, can I please stay home today?" She almost always said "Yes." I would smile, thank God then go back to bed. My elementary and secondary experiences with school were tragic, and should have been illegal. School was segregated–in every way: by race, by what officials defined as "intellectual capacity," by what we were taught (our books were literally two years old when we got them; we were at least two years behind our more affluent counterparts). I didn't need to go to school five days a week to learn what was being taught. Two or three days were enough for me to keep up and excel. Had I not had a mother who read to me, I could definitely have found myself as unsuccessful in school as the people of my case study. If neither the school nor the parents are preparing children to be successful in school, then of course they will not be.

Much later in life, I learned from my sisters that neither of our parents had been big proponents of "School." When my sisters were growing up, they had been given a choice to go to school or work. My mother, who graduated from college, was an avid reader, a gifted orator, and loved learning. But she had little faith in what School could do for us. This belief demonstrates just how little relevance School had (and continues to have today) in the lives of poor people. As a result, my mom passed on to me a love for education, but not for School.

The first book she read to me was the Bible. The stories of the Bible served as my bedtime stories. From listening to these stories I developed a deep sense of faith, a fantastical imagination, and a curiosity for creating things. These traits ultimately led me to my love for writing. If I'm having trouble making sense of some new concept, I write about it; and through writing about it, I build understanding.

From my father I developed a pension for critically analyzing everything and therefore a suspicion of the one called "God". When I was five years old, my father died. Before that, we were extremely close. He worked at night, so when I woke in the morning I would go and wait on our front porch for him to come home. My mother went off to work, and my father and I spent our days together. I followed him around the house, while he cleaned and made dinner for my sisters and mama and me. After he finished, I'd sit on his knee, while he stared into the silence of space. I don't remember us talking much, because we didn't need words to convey the dependence that we both had come to accept as *normal.* At naptime, I would lie back onto his chest, and he'd rub my belly until I fell asleep.

When he died, I continued my daily ritual of waiting for him for more than a year. With each day that I waited, my "favorite" sister and my mother would say: "I told you he's not coming. He's in heaven now with God." As a five-year-old, I wondered: "Who is this *god* that takes little five-year-old girls' daddies for no apparent reason and doesn't let them come home again?"

I didn't understand what it meant to "die." I was terribly unhappy; so I developed a wall around myself as I moved through a world that I decided, at five years old, was painful–my wall was *analysis.* I began to see the world as something to analyze, from a distance. I decided that it was best for me not to engage with the world through emotions, like love and loneliness, but the only way to travel through life was as an objective observer. This decision shaped my fascination with science.

After my father died, my family fell into abject poverty, which served to further confuse my little five-year-old mind. I didn't understand how I could be hungry and not have food. It didn't seem "natural" to me that one should have a physical need for something and the physical world not supply it. This experience fostered my interest in oppressed societies and therefore led me to my work as an anthropologist and therefore to this book.

The experiences we have within the first five years of our life are our introduction to the world. How we're introduced to the world shapes what I refer to as our "learning personality." Our personalities are made up of inherent qualities and external influences; likewise our *learning personality* is made up of processes that are natural and external controls that eventually come to feel like intuitive practices. For most of my life, I thought that I had a "natural" inclination toward organizing things. It seemed to come "natural" for me to think about how to put flesh on an idea. However, I began to notice that I also ironically dread the process. I later realized that organizing was not an inherent quality, but one that I developed from my childhood experiences with poverty and the confusion of death. Those encounters felt like chaos to me; therefore I responded to that chaos with order. Organization became an intuitive practice for me. It is part of my learning personality. I need an agenda to have a successful meeting. If there isn't one, I don't know what's been accomplished. So, as a teacher I designed my classroom to run the same way. I designed learning centers (before they were known as learning centers) and I posted each student's expectations in those centers, clearly visible for both the student and for me to see. It was a very productive classroom that almost ran itself.

A fellow teacher, on the other hand, was just the opposite. Her learning personality had been shaped by her experiences with classical music, which had been used to help her settle down into quietness. So she used classical music to help organize her classroom for engaging learning. It, too, was very effective. Another fellow teacher had been raised in a communal culture, where the women aggressively looked out for one another. She organized her classroom like a nurturing community. It too, delivered exceptional results.

Each of these classroom settings was effective because within them we also recognized the *learning personalities* of our students. I had one student who was diagnosed as attention deficit: "Tom." He literally could not sit still sometimes. He had a physical imbalance. So I would allow him to walk the circumference of the classroom to burn off some energy. I'd announce to the rest of the class (who were seventh graders): "Tom needs to burn some energy so that he can concentrate. Let's support him as he walks the room. Each of us will support him by not concentrating on what he's doing, but by concentrating on what we're doing. Stay focused on your own process."

Amazingly, these seventh graders would stay focused on their own process. Some were reading silently, some working in pairs on an assignment, some working in groups on a project. Tom would walk the room for about fifteen minutes. When he finished, he sat down and completed his assignments. Tom's *learning personality*, like many boys, included a need for physical exercise in order to do focused work with text exercises.

Most of the problems that schools experience with high-poverty, marginalized populations exist because there is no understanding of the concept of *learning personalities*, and a breakdown occurs in the communication between teachers and students and between the school and parents. This breakdown is exaggerated in the case of the families featured in this book, because their *learning personalities* were shaped by violence and a sense of "learned powerlessness," which has consequently engendered a cultural practice of educational failure in our inner-cities.

This cultural practice can best be explained through another concept at work–***the educational contract*– the subject of this book**. All schools have a "contract" with the parents of their students. Some charter and private schools have a literal contract that they require parents and students to sign before students are accepted into the program. In the case of charter schools, because they are state funded and therefore public schools, they can't legally not accept a child because parents don't agree with the contract. But if a parent has the mental wherewithal to seek out a charter school, s/he is generally not opposed to signing a contract that spells out the parent's responsibilities, the student's and the school's. Nevertheless, *all* schools have an unwritten, unspoken, but agreed upon *social contract*, or set of expectations for parents and for the school. But in poor schools with marginalized populations, no one seems to be aware of it. What's more, in these schools, the expectations of the "contract" are not shared among the different parties in the "contract."

For example, when I taught middle school, I had a practice in my classroom for dealing with misbehavior. If a student was acting out, I would stop in the middle of whatever was happening and call the child's parent, and have the parent talk to the child right then and there in the moment. I rarely used this practice because generally there was no need. I had set my classroom up so that it was so engaging, students complained when they had to leave for their next class. Once when I employed my famous practice of stopping the class to call the mother of a student who was interrupting the learning of the others, the mother said to me: "Is he at school? Is he in class? To which I answered: yes and yes. Then she said: "Then why are you calling me?"

That statement symbolizes the attitudes of too many of our parents given the type of school we had. In this school (which was in all respects a charter school before charter schools existed) we had some of the best parents in a public school system, but they did not have the same understanding about their role in the school as we had about their role in the school. When our school was threatened, they were there to protect us. They understood their power as a parent group and they used it very effectively; and they expected us as the school to be totally and completely responsible for *all* the learning that occurs with their children. Furthermore, it was expected that anything their children needed while at school—that included meals; uniforms; school supplies; behavior; and learning: exposure to new ideas, new places, class work, and, ironically, homework—the school provided it. The attitude was: If children are not performing well in school, it is solely the school's fault. This is a common expectation of parents of urban schools of color across the United States.

Consequently, schools have become less accountable to children and their families, and more answerable to test scores. This shift in accountability has impacted the way learning happens in the classroom. In too many urban classrooms, teaching is composed of endless practice tests on printed worksheets. In extreme cases, we have seen school staff so much more focused on test scores than on the children to the point where they helped students cheat on the tests, such as the cheating scandal in Atlanta in 2011. One hundred and seventy eight educators in forty-four of the district's 100 schools were involved in the students cheating on standardized tests—often with the approval of high-level administrators. Thirty-five educators were indicted on criminal charges. Atlanta was a severe case with more than a hundred staff involved, but this pressure to help students pass tests that they are not prepared to pass is a more common occurrence in public schools across the United States than one might imagine. When schools are held accountable to students (instead of to test scores), education is made valuable to the student. No "teacher" would help a student cheat on a test, rather than ensure the student actually knows the information. I have enclosed "teacher" in quotations to emphasize the inherent qualities of that title. A teacher is what my student described in the "Acknowledgements" of this book: It is someone who inspires her students to engage with the humanity of their conscience and to become better human beings. A teacher is someone who reaches out to his students in profoundly impactful ways to stir up their passions and support their pursuit of them. A teacher excites her students to the idea of learning and to nurture that idea. A "teacher" would never harm his/her students by cheating on a test in order to save their job.

However, when parents are absent from the school, the school loses focus on the important details of ensuring high performance from students. To ensure that students perform well on state and national tests, rather than helping students cheat on those tests, teachers should first of all be able to pass their own certified tests. As I demonstrate in the final Chapter, in many high-poverty, low-performing schools, it is not uncommon for more than forty percent of the teachers in these schools to have failed their own performance exams to obtain their teacher's certification. According to the Education Trust, as many as forty one percent of the math classes in underserved schools are taught by teachers with neither a certificate or major in that field. Secondly, teachers and administrators must be taught how to deliver curriculum to students in high-poverty, marginalized communities. For example, I was working with an elementary school in one of the largest school districts in the country to help teachers improve the reading scores of fifth graders. An administrator who was in charge of the professional development of "reading" teachers in the entire district said: "The problem with these kids is they don't know how to think. And that's not something you can teach them.

They either know how to do it, or they don't." That was a shocking statement.

The supervisor responsible for helping teachers understand how to teach children in the fourth largest school district in the nation to read believed that a child is either *inherently* able to perform critical thinking exercises or not. As I outline in Chapters 3 and 4, skills like critical thinking and problem solving are skills that are explicitly taught to children from the day they come home from the hospital as infants. It is details like these that the school loses focus of when the parents (the direct customers of such practices) aren't screaming as loud as they can to expose such egregious practices to the world. These details are traded-in, in favor of the big picture of performance numbers (meaning, just the "test scores" themselves). As a consequence, we see "so called" teachers and educators helping students cheat on tests, and in effect, trade in their students' human rights to have a quality education for high test scores. High test scores and a quality education *should* be synonymous, not in conflict.

When I arrived in Houston, I encountered the same parental behavior that I experienced in New York City. It is a behavior that has become part of a national cultural practice—it is a social script that has defined American public education over the past fifty years. No amount of school reform has made much of a difference in student performance in large urban schools of color...because we (the education community) have given up on the parents. We have decided that there's nothing we can do to control their participation, but we have the kids and we can work with them. So we have spent millions of dollars to reform our way of teaching and learning, and it has not made much of a difference. We must turn our attention to the parents and the households of our students, while continuing to reform our schools.

Please do not misunderstand me. I do believe that major reforms need to occur in our public schools. For example, school systems across the U.S. are in a battle with parents and nonprofit groups over standardized testing. Personally, I am a big proponent of standardization of education. However, in the U.S. we standardize content and assessments, but we do not standardize teacher quality or education funding. Recently, a state district court in Texas ruled that the way the state funds its public schools is unconstitutional, both because the money is insufficient and because it is not distributed fairly.

How are students supposed to perform to standardized assessments when quality of teachers and funding is so drastically different? We must change the practice of putting the least experienced teachers in schools with the highest academic needs. And it is imperative that we implement on-going professional development that is designed to keep our schools in step with the advancements of our society (much of the professional development that teachers currently receive in urban public schools of color is inadequate in the eyes of everyone involved).

We also need to have higher standards–children will rise up as high as they are challenged to rise. The Obama Administration conducted studies that revealed that children who receive math in the lower grades do much better in math in the high school grades; however only forty percent of black and Latino children receive math in the lower grades. This is a set up. And it is unacceptable and must be changed by our school system.

We should create more relevant assessment processes for students, teachers and administrators. As teachers we should not be afraid to have our work assessed by how well our students perform because that is the only thing that tells us that we have accomplished our task–which is student achievement. AND we should not forget to include parents as a critical component in the formula to fix our schools. When parents are present in our schools, we all feel more accountable to the institutional reforms.

THE INTRODUCTION

No amount of school reform is going to close the achievement gap between black and white students if we continue to exclude parents from these reform efforts. There are several non-profits working to establish reform measures with parents. But there has been few to no federal or state institutional reform actions that target parent participation in the school lives of children. The Obama Administration has recently allotted thirty million dollars to one such program: The Promise Neighborhoods Program. However, given the gravity of the situation, that's just a drop in the bucket. The Promise Neighborhoods Program is based on the work of the Harlem Children's Zone, where parents and children are surrounded with services (both social and academic) from the time the child is born through the child's career (cradle to career).

My research authenticates the need for similar programs. I have confirmed that the achievement gap between black and white students doesn't begin at school, but by age two. Based on my research, it is my proposal that the academic difference is not based in the physiology of students (it is not a biological-racial issue), because it is not something that exists at birth. It is something that is developed. Therefore the gap is a social issue. Yet, as a nation, we seek an academic solution to this social problem.

A social problem is one that is made up collective influences such as traditions, customs, history, values, beliefs and certain available knowledge. A Washington DC judge who works closely with inner-city single mothers told me this story: One of the young African-American mothers in the judge's program had had a child at a very young age (as an early teen). But the young woman had made a significant effort to do everything she "knew" to do in order to ensure her child was well cared for and ready for school. The young woman was heartbroken when she took her child to school on the first day, where she learned that she was supposed to have already taught her child the alphabet, numbers, shapes and colors. The judge said, with sincere compassion: "She just didn't know." The knowledge that was available to this young mother and millions of other parents like her has placed their children at a significant disadvantage academically.

I was taken aback as I discovered how this disadvantaged position came to be in African-American communities across our nation. I found that the historic 1954 U.S. Supreme Court case *Brown v. the Board of Education of Topeka Kansas* contributes to attitudes that engender this academic inequality between black and white students. And I show in Chapter 1 how this case contributes to this disparity, which actually begins to take form the day that babies are brought home from the hospital.

Discovering "America"

I arrived in Houston, Texas in the summer of 2003. I had recently completed all of my coursework in my PhD anthropology program, and was searching for a location to do my fieldwork. Prior to coming to Texas, I spent three years traveling every summer and winter to some part of southern Africa or Latin America to conduct research. I've spent time in Cape Town, Pretoria and Johannesburg (all in South Africa); Blantyre and Lilongwe in Malawi; Chiapas in Mexico; and in Cuba.

I was exploring the educational system of each place and was considering conducting my fieldwork in one these locations. The educational system of these regions seemed ripe for research–particularly the South African system (the control of which had been recently transferred from the white Afrikaans minority population). There were an overwhelming number of black African children living on the street–who had lost their parents to the AIDS epidemic and who were doing odd jobs in between periods of begging. The new South African government, the African National Congress (ANC), was grappling with how to educate these youngsters and deal honestly with the fact that they were probably the family's only source of income. The South African situation was dire. But, astoundingly, not as dire as the educational situation I encountered in the United States in Houston, TX.

I stumbled upon the dismal educational condition in Houston through a reading program sponsored by the pastor of a small church. She hosts this program every summer for the children of her church and the surrounding community, colloquially known as *The Bottoms*, in the Third Ward of Houston. *The Bottoms* is a black working-poor-class community on the border of Downtown Houston, which over the past decade has become a very expensive place to live. The Bottoms is surrounded by some of the most expensive neighborhoods in Houston; yet, it is one of the poorest areas in the City. At the time of this research, it was at "the bottom" of the City's list of resources, development, services, and street repairs. The area is an enigma of urban rural confluences. It is populated with small shotgun houses– some without the traditional pleasures of urban living, like running water and electricity; incredibly narrow blacktop streets that are bounded on both sides by very, very deep trenches, which are designed to catch the rain water that can come down in torrents like a tropical rain storm (but more often than not catches cars that have backed up too far and fallen in); and some of the worst performing schools in Houston. Most of the residents are renters and they dream of moving away to a "better" neighborhood, even while developers are at auctions looking for unpaid taxes in that area like hawks waiting for prey to die in a desert. The neighborhood's location,

5

less than a mile from the center of downtown Houston, offers a spectacular view of the downtown skyline.

The pastor of the small church which is embedded in the heart of this community is a big advocate for education, and about three-fourths of the children in the community that surrounds her church do not read at grade level. So, she took action and created this reading program. The summer of 2003, I arrived in the middle of it. There were about fifty children attending, which was a striking accomplishment, given the size of the congregation of the church. One of the program leaders had gone through the neighborhood and gathered up children who were sitting around doing nothing.

The ages of the fifty children ranged from four to seventeen. Of those fifty children, only two could read–a six- and a nine-year-old. They were prolific readers. The nine-year-old is the son of the pastor. The other approximately forty-eight children could not read. I'm not talking about comprehension, which is what educators generally mean when they say someone can't read– they're reading the letters or the symbols (which is what linguists would call letters) but they don't understand anything they've read–that's a comprehension problem. These forty-eight kids, some as old as seventeen, could

6

not even read the symbols–they weren't capable of the most basic reading skill known as phonics. I was stunned.

I was taken aback because in all my travels to under-developed communities in Africa and Latin America, I had not come across children who were actually attending school and who were in middle and high school grades that couldn't phonetically read the symbols of the alphabet. I thought back to the moment I met the families in South Africa, who were sometimes sacrificing food to pay for their children to attend school, and wondered why families in the United States were so seemingly lackadaisical regarding education. I also wondered why Cuba (whose economic GDP per capita at that time was about $2700) had an illiteracy rate of less than two percent, but the U.S. (whose GDP per capita at that time was more than $25,000) would have entire communities across the country like the one in Third Ward Houston.

But these "why" questions just led me to more and more complex "why" questions, which did not lead to any real answers. Anthropologists are taught to ask "how." By asking "How did this situation come to be?" I began to plow through the nature of the condition, and I slowly became a part of the community. It was not a strategic move on my part, although participant observation is a mainstay research method for anthropologists. Initially, I did not approach this problem as a researcher. I had an array of emotions that began to flow. Having grown up in a similarly situated community to *The Bottoms*, I was heartbroken and angry by what was clearly negligence.

The experience reminded me too much of my own childhood. I grew up in West Dallas (Dallas, TX), a community that was so poor other poor communities made fun of us. Underprivileged people all over Dallas dreaded the idea of becoming so poverty-stricken that they would be reduced to living in West Dallas. The schools were *way* below "low performing." Most of our teachers had extremely low expectations for us as students. I remember, in high school, some of my classmates were being called down to the guidance counselor's office to talk about college opportunities. Fortunately, our guidance counselor had grown up in a similar condition of racism and was doing her best to ensure we had opportunities that she had not had. However, for some reason, I was not being called down to talk to the counselor, despite the fact that I was graduating in the top ten percent of my class. As my classmates

8

were going down to talk to the counselor, I said to my teacher: "I need to go talk to the counselor." The teacher said to me: "But you said you didn't want to go to college". I responded with: "I've changed my mind."

She was referring to an off-handed comment I had made earlier that year, which I had really made because I just didn't see how I could afford to go to college; furthermore, because of teachers like her, I hated school and I couldn't imagine prolonging what seemed like torture to me. But my teacher's response was: "You don't need to go to college...I don't know why you feel like you need to go to college just because your friends are going...bla bla bla bla bla..." At the "bla bla" point I stopped hearing her, so I'm not exactly sure what came after that. I was disappointed to hear an educator tell me that I didn't need to continue my education, while telling us about how her children were going to the best schools in Dallas.

In spite of my high school experiences with questionable "educators" and a dubious education, I received offers from University of Texas at Austin and Southern Methodist University, two of the most prestigious schools in Texas and Dallas, respectively. I toured one of the schools (SMU), but I felt out of place. I didn't understand how to engage with the possibility of what attending this school with less than one percent of its population being black could mean for me; and no one ever encouraged me to accept those offers. So I didn't. It was ten years before I developed the acumen on my own to enroll in college. As a consequence, I have consistently found myself ten years behind my peers. I applied to Columbia University in New York City. I was accepted and given a scholarship for more than fifty percent of my tuition and fees.

As I remembered these moments, I experienced them all over again while I was with the children in *The Bottoms*. They were excited every year in August as they prepared to go "back to school" after the summer break. They talked about the clothes and shoes they wanted for "back-to-school," the classes they hoped to get and the teachers they hoped not to get, and the best schools for their unique interests. It was no different from the conversations that children of middle-class, upper-middle-class and upper-class families might have about an annual event that has a profound and significant impact in the lives of the entire family and community.

My confusion lay in not knowing with whom to place my disappointment or to lay blame. Almost a decade earlier, five colleagues and I started a school in New York

City. The students of our school were just like these children in Third Ward Houston. Yet, we had succeeded in helping the New York youngsters exceed the required state and national standards. So whose fault was it that these kids in Third Ward Houston couldn't read? Was it the schools'? The parents'? The culture's? The kids' themselves? The breakdown of the community? The intrusion of crack cocaine? Each of these elements has been blamed in various research studies over the past six decades.

It all seemed too complicated, so rather than spend precious time locating fault (or even researching the genesis of this crisis in their educational processes), I started a program that addressed the immediate need of teaching the kids to read. I developed a tutorial program that consisted of a partnership with the University of Houston and three public schools in Third Ward. I trained and placed English majors in the classrooms of those schools to tutor their most academically challenged students. The first semester, seventeen university students registered for the class. I placed them in our partner schools: Blackshear Elementary, Ryan Middle, and Jack Yates High.

It was through this program that I began to consciously observe the academic behavioral patterns of the students, the teachers, the systemic processes of the school as an institution, and how parents engaged with all of these. I soon discovered that I had sort of fallen into my dissertation research study. I began to deliberately use the tools of anthropology to move through the process of understanding how we were losing an entire generation of youth right in front of our eyes.

I wanted to know how more than 5,000 African American students in this community could be attending school and doing so poorly in the most basic purpose of school—learning to read. As I waded through previous solutions proposed by politicians, school administrators, parents, and researchers, I discovered some very insightful proposals that had great potential for change. And yet, there were no overall changes. So I began to look at language—first at how it was used in talking about the problem, then how it was used to perpetuate the problem; and I found a very interesting phenomenon at work. I learned that how we are introduced to the world has everything to do with how we learn. Through participant observation, I examined the "home-life" of three different families, and tracked how what newborn babies came home to from the hospital was contributing to the children's performance in school.

Let Me Introduce You to "America"

The first family, who I am calling "the Freeman family," represents roughly sixty-five percent of the families in *The Bottoms*, and they are a compilation of about five different actual families. This group is my primary research case. The Freemans are a black family, who lived and attended schools in *The Bottoms* and can be categorized in the socio-economic class of the "working-poor." I followed this family closely, yet casually, over a period of two years, during which I spent time in each of the schools the children attended, from elementary to high school. By "casual," I mean I was generally in the school to assist teachers through my tutorial program, not to record classes or do formal interviews. I conducted a number of informal interviews and never used a recorder because of the school personnel's paranoia, generated by the low student test scores.

The administrative office that supervised these schools made it clear that everybody's job was on the line. For example, when the children returned to the middle school for the 2004-05 school year, ninety percent of the staff, including teachers and administrators (from the principal to the receptionist) were "not rehired" (the term they used). The entire school staff was forced to re-apply for their jobs–and only ten were invited back. Those ten were re-assigned to new positions, including the principal who was re-assigned to an assistant principal's position. She had only been at the school for one year before this event. Several of the teachers were convinced that I was spying on them for the District.

The elementary school (whose principal was the most open and frank with me) and the high school went through the same process, as student scores dropped them to the bottom of the rankings. In fact, over the past seven years since the completion of this research, each of these schools have gone through several of these complete overhaul changes where the entire staff from the principal to the janitor is released and a whole new staff is brought in to reorganize or reconstitute the school. Yet, no real change has occurred from the time of conducting this research until seven years later at the publication of this research.

I also followed the Freeman family to church, home, and the streets. By "streets," I mean their recreation was generally just hanging out outside in the park or literally in the street. I designed two educational programs sponsored by and held at their church. I took the children on recreational and academic trips to museums, libraries, and conservation parks. I spent only five short periods of observation in their home. I did not spend more time in their home because I was often stood up. When I arrived for scheduled home visits, no one would answer the door. However, when I arrived for scheduled appointments to take the children out, there was always a response. I felt overwhelmed by what became a self-imposed responsibility to expose the children to other ways of being. With or without me, the children were rarely home. They desperately looked for other places to be. Unless there was some program or person taking them on trips, they generally just hung out "in the streets" until late into the night.

The comparative case studies were conducted over the same time period and include an upper middle-class African American family and an upper middle-class Anglo family. The African American family, who I am calling "the Strivers," live only a mile and a half away from the Freemans. The Strivers represent a bordering neighborhood, and they are a compilation of about seven different actual families. Angela Strivers pastors the church that the Freemans attend and owns several properties in Third Ward, some of which are in *The Bottoms*.

I spent two years working with Angela developing educational programs for the children of the community, and building systemic processes to support better functioning systems within their real estate business. During the two years of this research, I lived in one of the Strivers' properties, and helped out occasionally with their son. I was therefore, deeply embedded in the family's life. I experienced the day-to-day rituals of everything from getting their son up and off to school to the daily bedtime rituals that concluded the day. In watching the drastic differences of these home rituals between the Strivers and the Freemans, I could not help but link the rituals to the performance of the kids in school, which were clearly connected. Therefore, I looked at two African American families to answer the questions of why some children of color do well, while others do not, and why so many children of color across the nation are having what seems like the same kind of problem in school.

The Anglo family, that I am calling "the Mann family," worked and attended school less than a mile away from *The Bottoms* at the University of Houston (UH). The Manns represent the "ideal" American family and consist of about four different actual families. I met this family while working at UH through the partnership I developed to place tutors in the public schools in Third Ward.

The Mann family provides a base from which I work to understand what is going on. I use this base because in my research I found that all school reform efforts (government, non-profit, and private efforts) use this central place to determine reform programs. They use this foundational position as the "norm" that they try to mimic in schools that are considered to be outside of the "norm"–outside of mainstream culture. They call the populations of these schools "minorities," despite the fact that these populations now make up the majority of Americans. I further felt compelled to consider this base when I came across an important American text–the *Declaration of Independence*. I made this discovery while researching the history of school in this country and how school was designed to create a sense of "normalcy" that over the past generations of the existence of the country, had sought to ally itself with "nature." The document begins with "We hold these *truths* to be *self-evident"* (my emphasis in italics). Such a statement implies that what is about to be put forth is truth, and that the truth is obvious, it is visible, and it is non-negotiable–it is part of a "natural order." A "natural order" suggests inherent qualities in nature, which some believe are designed by God. This belief is authenticated in America's history through policies that categorized black Americans as non-citizens and, more egregiously, as non-human, according to the "natural order." Therefore, educational policies that marginalized African Americans were considered "natural."

My discovery of this information prompted me to return to memories where I experienced the devastation of what it means to be outside of this "naturalized" identity. The process of becoming a part of a naturalized community looks for inscriptions on one's consciousness and even on the body that are often painful to take on or endure. Imagine, if you can, what it is like to function in a society that for hundreds of years did not see you as "human." For me, growing up in the South of the United States in the late 1960s and early 1970s, that thought was present every day in the formative years of shaping my worldview. It permeated my decisions, my expectations, my goals and my dreams (they were extremely limited–limited only to the visions that my parents could pass on).

However, when I was in the 7th grade, we were bussed to the north side of town to attend a school with a predominant white population. The experience was part of the efforts to integrate schools, which was mandated as a result of *Brown vs. Board of Education of Topeka Kansas.* The first time I saw the homes of those students, while riding through their neighborhood in our big yellow bus, it occurred to me that I had to create new goals for myself. I had never seen anything like that before. I remember thinking: "Wow. I need new dreams."

I went on to create those new dreams for myself and to bring them to fruition. Yet, thirty-one years after that realization, I continue to encounter racist behavior that argues with me about my worth as a black woman. For example, I walked into a barbershop owned and operated by Asians in the African American community where I lived in Houston, TX, to get my hair cut. The man at the desk was surly and unpleasant. It bothered me, because this is the South and everybody is polite (even if they're about to cut your throat, it is not uncommon for them to say please). But I ignored his attitude because the haircut was only $3.00. Actually they advertise the price (which is also the name of the shop) at $2.99. I spoke to him, but he did not speak back. I ignored it, because the haircut is only $3.00, and I thought this is just how he is (maybe it's a cultural thing, I reasoned). However, two white women walked into the shop, and he greeted them with smiles and small talk I didn't even know he could do in English: "Hello. How are you? Good to see you today," he said. They ignored his pleasantries and said: We wanna get haircuts." He immediately seated them in a barber's chair and then seated me afterwards (even though I walked in first and had been there long enough to be sitting in the waiting area). The two white women finished with their haircuts and went to the desk to pay. They each paid $3.00. He thanked them with smiles. They ignored him and walked out of the door. When I went to pay, he said: "$5.00". I was confused and at a loss. And I began to experience a mixture of anger and pain. Then I found myself shaking. He had rattled and disoriented me. The sign says $2.99. Everybody else paid $3.00, but he's charging me $5.00. I explained that to him. He said: "That's for men. Women pay $5.00." I said: "The two women ahead of me paid only $3.00." He said:

"You had more cut." At the time, I had a cut like a man—nearly bald, which I pointed out to him. I also pointed out that the white women had a lot more hair than me. So, in frustration he said with a slight pitch of yelling in his tone: "Ok. $3.00 then!"

This encounter, along with my high school teacher telling me that I didn't need to go to college, represent the gamut of emotions that I experience as a black woman in this country. These practices suggest that in order for me to be accepted in the "natural" order of things that I must endure painful inscriptions to change my identity—essentially I cannot be acceptable as I am. And, not unlike the subjects of my primary case, any problem I come across (in the case of this research, in education) is because there is something inherently (biologically) wrong with me (such as, my brain is inferior because it's small, as George Morton claimed about people of color in his scientific research that came to be known as scientific racism. I tell more of this research in Chapter 4).

Therefore, I decided to add these comparison studies to show two things: 1) the problem of low performing students is not simply a race problem, because not all black students are performing poorly; but 2) the problem is situated in race. By that I mean, children who are performing poorly in school are not doing so simply because they are black; however, forty-five percent of the kids who are failing school are African American. Therefore, the problem has to be *embedded* in the cultural history of what it means to be black in this country, which means the problem is located in the dilemma that we have with race.

I realize there is a danger in presenting so few families as representatives of whole groups. But I believe, based on my two years of observations, the issues that I have chosen to address can be demonstrated in these families. It was not my intention to present the Mann family or those it stands for as the enemy to African American families. My intention was to show the complexity of race relations in this country that was built on legalized racial discrimination against those of African descent, and which refuses, as a country, to acknowledge or recognize the lasting vestiges of such a system and deal honestly and deeply with the people it has affected.

CHAPTER 1

The Educational Contract

The difficulty in explaining why some African American students do so poorly in school, is explaining why their parents allow them to fail. In a formal interview with the principal of Blackshear Elementary School about parent participation, he told me this story. It was just one of many that he shared:

Principal: Justin, a fourth grader, cussed out his teacher, twice. I called his home and his step-father answered the phone. I explained that Justin cussed out his teacher after she spoke to him about hitting a classmate who was looking at him. The step-father said, "Put him on the phone." There was a series of "imos": "imo git chu when you git home" (translated: I'm going to get you when you get home). That was it. Justin went back to class. The next day, he had the same problem. I called home again. The mother was at work. The step-father answered. And the process continued. I now have Justin sitting outside my office, to take away the possibility of other children looking at him and distracting him. I wrote this letter to his parents. What's missing? Neither parent came to the school. After two days of being away from his class, Justin decided that he wanted to return to it, where his teacher is "stupid" and the kids are looking at him. I said "You need to do your work". Justin responded: "I don't care what chu say. I'm going back to class." I said, "You need to do your work". I called home again. The step-father threatened him. Justin wanted me to call his mom. I refused. His step-father threatened him again. He finally sat down and did work. When you were a kid, could you have cussed out your teacher, and then went to the office, disrespected your principal, and said, "I wanna call my mama"?

Researcher: No

Principal: Why not? Because your mama would have come to the school with her belt. Justin's mom supports what he does.

This story epitomizes what the principal called an "addiction to entitlement" and an "abdication of responsibility" and it described over sixty-five percent of the students and parents of this school, the middle, and the high school in *The Bottoms* at the time of this research. My initial response to this behavior was one of conflict. I lived in this community for more than two years and I knew some of these parents. I knew them to be well-meaning parents who sincerely loved their children, who wanted the best for their children (but had no idea what that meant or how to give it to them).

I could appreciate their dilemma because of my own experience where my class was bussed to another part of the city and I was able to see how "the best" was defined outside of my community. So, as I listened to this principal vent (quite intellectually, sometimes correctly, but mostly offensively) about these parents refusing to take their share of the responsibility for their children's learning, I wondered how exactly we got here? How was it that these parents could genuinely love their children and yet behave in such a way that would suggest they regretted ever giving birth? Their behavior towards the school was as if the school was bothering them when they got phone calls for help in modifying their children's behavior. They seemed pissed off when teachers asked them to check their children's homework. They "wanted the best" for their children, yet their children arrived at school on their very first day at four years old completely lost on things they should have learned by the time they were two years old; and their children repeatedly showed up to class unprepared for the day of learning. They were unprepared academically, emotionally, and even physically (kids were often hungry).

Outsourcing Education

In graduate school I came across a theory known as "social contract theory." It seemed to be at work here, but no one appeared to be aware of it. The lack of awareness was working against both the parents' and the schools' best interests. The theory began to surface in the eighteenth century from French philosopher Jean-Jacques Rousseau in his book *On the Social Contract*.

The theory became the cornerstone of modern political and social thought. Rousseau argues that societies are formed to fulfill our human needs. In these societies we form partnerships in which we choose to give up part of our freedom in exchange for goods and services. We enter into an unwritten *social contract* that is recognized by all who are involved, in which we agree to follow the rules of authority in order to get something we want. For example, we agree to partner in the rule of *mandatory schooling* in exchange for publicly funded education. We agree that the School, as an institution, should be the authority on this subject. Consequently, we enter into a social contract with the School–thus, we enter into an *educational contract*. The *contract* is not something that anybody signs and usually is not overtly acknowledged, but it is understood–If I give up certain freedoms, I get certain resources from the government.

This idea was popular with early American leaders George Washington and Thomas Jefferson, who used it to advocate for a national public education system supported by federal or state taxes. Jefferson argued that in order to have a true democracy, Americans required certain basic skills that included reading, writing, and rhetoric. However, because most of those who made up America at that time did not possess those skills, and were therefore incapable of teaching their children, Jefferson argued that we should provide public schooling for every child. In essence, he was suggesting a form of *outsourcing* that responsibility to a more capable entity. Jefferson was concerned that uneducated citizens would lead to uninformed citizens who could not be truly free and make rational decisions about the nation, and would consequently become pawns of political whims. His bill did not pass, but in the nineteenth century his views captured the sentiment of the American public and polity.

"This...value placed on equality among the classes noted during the late colonial period continued as the nation developed. The eloquent voices of educational reformers were heard throughout the nineteenth and twentieth century in support of public education and equality of opportunity. In the mid 1800s there was the leadership of Horace Mann and Henry Barnard. Mann's vision of the common school led to the development of a public school system in almost every state by 1860." (Hiatt, 1994).

Critics of urban schools of color often blame parents for "outsourcing" their responsibility to the school. However, there is a long tradition, for most Americans, of practicing that custom in our nation. For black Americans that custom was significantly delayed. It was not until after the historic 1954 US Supreme Court case *Brown v. the Board of Education of Topeka Kansas* that the practice became available to African Americans. The *Brown* case signified a cultural reconstruction project of huge proportions. It successfully ended legal segregation in education in the United States, and laid the groundwork to dismantle segregation in areas such as housing, transportation, voting, employment and public accommodations. It is viewed as the most significant case on race in America's history. On May 17, 1954, US Supreme Court Chief Justice Earl Warren announced that:

Today education is perhaps the most important function of state and local governments. Compulsory school attendance laws and the great expenditures for education both demonstrate our recognition of the importance of education to our democratic society. It is required in the performance of our most basic public responsibilities, even service in the armed forces. It is the very foundation of good citizenship. Today it is a principal instrument in awakening the child to cultural values, in preparing him for later professional training, and in helping him to adjust normally to his environment. In these days, it is doubtful that any child may reasonably be expected to succeed in life if he is denied the opportunity of an education. Such an opportunity, where the state has undertaken to provide it, is a right, which must be made available to all on equal terms. We come then to the question presented: Does segregation of children in public schools solely on the basis of race, even though the physical facilities and other "tangible" factors may be equal, deprive the children of the minority group of equal educational opportunities? We believe that it does. (*Brown*, 347 U.S. 483, 493)

The passing of this decision not only made the Jeffersonian education reform ideology of universal education possible for African Americans, but also validated their expectation to be able to, like all Americans had since the 1860s, expect that the public school system would now handle the responsibility that they, like their Anglo counterparts, were not capable of handling. African Americans, too, could now *outsource* that responsibility to a more capable entity.

Opponents of the *Brown* case declared that there would be violence, withdrawal of white students from integrated schools, and black students with lower IQs that are inherent to being black would be enrolled into white schools. Furthermore, it was believed that enrolling black students in white schools would cause venereal diseases to spread, and there would be an increase of "illegitimate" children enrolled in white schools. Their point was that integration would destroy their way of life because black children and their families were genetically inferior at all levels, including cognitive, physical, social, and spiritual levels. Moreover, black Americans are not actually "Americans," but more egregiously not worthy of being recognized or respected as human.

This ideology, or belief, was rooted and historically legitimated in previous laws of the land. For example, in 1787 politicians wanted to be able to count slaves (people of African descent) in their state for the purposes of determining the number of House representatives they would get in Congress. The number of House representatives each state gets is based on the population of the state, unlike the Senate, in which each state gets two senators regardless of the size of the state.

In order to increase the number of representatives in the House, politicians wanted to include the slaves in their state in the population count. However, they did not want to give slaves citizenship. The compromise was to count slaves as "three-fifths of a man."

Before this law, for nearly four hundred years, blacks in this country were not considered human at all; they were considered as chattel. In 1857, the *Dred Scott v. Sanford Ruling* by the U.S. Supreme Court ruled that people of African descent brought into the United States and held as slaves (or their descendants, whether or not they were slaves) were not protected by the Constitution and were not U.S. citizens. The Court went on to conclude that slaves, as chattel or private property, could not be taken away from their owners without due process. And although, in 1868, after the American Civil War, one of the Reconstruction Amendments was the Fourteenth Amendment that granted citizenship to: "All persons born or naturalized in the United States," thereby granting citizenship to former slaves, the law did not change the prevailing belief of American nationalism, which is deeply rooted in a history that at one point defined blacks as *three-fifths of a person*. In other words, the nationalist ideology of Americanism was that blacks were not fully human and certainly not American. This ideology is what drove and authenticated the *Brown* ruling. However, the *Brown* ruling lost its focus in the implementation process

Outsourcing Children

The Civil Rights Movement, which drove the *Brown* ruling, was about equal access to the same resources for all citizens. The *social contract* of our nation was severely biased in favor of white Americans. The Civil Rights Movement sought to equalize the *contract*, given that African Americans were taxed at the same rate as their white brothers and sisters. However, somehow the fight for equal rights was distorted into a fight for "integration." It was in this alteration of the struggle that education for black students began to go drastically wrong. In complete dissimilarity to the intended outcome of the *Brown* case, young African American parents in large urban inner-city schools began to see their role in their children's school lives relegated only to ensuring attendance.

The trajectory of this path is winding and a bit complex (so please bear with me for a moment). Though not the central focus of this book, it is critical to understanding how in the 1960s and 70s the Black Power Movement was unfolding parallel to the Civil Rights Movement. The Black Power Movement took a more militant path to achieving equal rights. As a consequence, there were extremely volatile moments across the nation, with many of those moments ending in black Americans destroying their own neighborhoods. When I was working in the newsroom of New York Newsday in 1991, we saw the same scenario happening again after the Rodney King trial ended with a verdict that exonerated the police officers who were caught on video ruthlessly beating Mr. King who was face down on the ground. Los Angeles erupted in violence. Black residents were burning down the houses they lived in and destroying the stores in their neighborhoods.

My Anglo colleagues in the newsroom could not understand it. They asked every African American in the newsroom: "Why would they destroy their own neighborhood?" Some African Americans in the newsroom felt overwhelmed by having to explain such a seemingly "nonsensical" act—Where are they going to live now? They've burned down their houses. It was clear to me, as someone who had grown up in a similar neighborhood—

where we didn't own any of the businesses; where the food stores had so little respect for us that the goods they sold were so damaged they would have been thrown into the trash in more affluent neighborhoods; where furniture merchants sold us products that were so cheaply made that they were nearly unusable long before we ever paid off the exorbitant payment plan (with exaggerated interest rates that were unheard of outside of our community)–It was clear to me that they were burning down the houses they lived in because they were shacks that they rented from people who would never have lived in anything so wretched themselves. These "slumlords" thought of the people who did live in their shacks as animals. Ironically, the residents' behavior during these riot experiences inadvertently served to confirm the owners' beliefs while the residents were trying to send a different message: that they were tired of being thought of as animals. They would not live that way anymore. They would be freed of those bonds, even if it meant they would have no place to live.

This Los Angeles neighborhood is a product of what happened when "integration" replaced the fight for "equality" in the 1970s. At the end of that period,

African Americans made significant strides in expanding access to parts of the country that had been previously closed off, such as schools, universities, jobs and neighborhoods. A select few black Americans, who were prepared to "integrate" into mainstream American culture (i.e. white American customs, practices, and neighborhoods), began to move out of black neighborhoods, which as a consequence began to deteriorate. The neighborhoods reached a "tipping point". Malcolm Gladwell, in his book of the same name, defines a tipping point as "the moment of critical mass, the threshold, the boiling point." He argues that change quickly and unexpectedly occurs when enough people buy into an idea to "tip" the scales in a different direction. However, he contends that the percentage needed to tip the scales in a different direction is pretty small. For example, he documents how a neighborhood drastically changes when only about twenty percent of the residents change.

He shows with empirical evidence that if only about twenty percent of the residents of a neighborhood are professionals, then that community will be a desirable place to live. However, if less than twenty percent of the residents are professionals, then the neighborhood will depreciate. He argues that having examples of professionals living in a neighborhood offers other residents (particularly children) hope that success is attainable. After African Americans won the fight for "integration" in the 1970s, most of the professionals moved out of black neighborhoods, leaving them to decline. By the 1980s, crack cocaine found its way into black neighborhoods and rendered them utterly incapacitated

Public schools in these neighborhoods today are the consequence of parents that either lived through this deterioration or were born into it. Therefore, these parents are less equipped to participate in their children's education than their Anglo, middle and upper economic class counterparts, because they have never experienced a quality education themselves. In light of that reality, they relinquished *all* of their parental functions as it relates to education over to the *School*, which contradicts what the principal at the beginning of this chapter suggested. This *"abandonment"* of their responsibility was not initially an act of negligence on these parents' part, but rather an act of trust in a system that had been known to provide access to opportunity to its constituents. Nonetheless, this new ideological possibility of being able to relinquish that responsibility to the School precipitated a misunderstanding about parents' responsibilities and structured the next six decades of conversations following the *Brown* decision about education in large, poor, urban schools of color.

Powerful "Victims"

Brown v. the Board of Education of Topeka initiated a new expectation for African American parents and for the School as an institution. The country admitted that it had miserably failed U.S. citizens of African descent, and their inability to compete academically was not some genetic trait inherent to being black. This admission did two things. One, it inadvertently created a "victim" category for African Americans–a category that some have overused. The language around this category undermines the language of survival that is reminiscent of the history of black peoples in this country. A "victim" is one with no power to change his/her circumstances. A victim is "controlled" by the whims of popular discourse. The parents of my primary case study often said: "There's nothing I can do about what's happening." They told me how they felt they could not change the way the schools operate in their community. The only thing they thought they could do was put their children in a "better" school. However, the "better" schools often have long waiting lists. So they resign to believing that they are powerless to change their circumstances.

The second thing the *Brown* case did, ironically, was position African American parents in an important place in the power structure of the relationship between parents and the School. Foucault (1978) argues that power comes from below and it is exercised from infinite points in an unequal interplay of constantly changing relations. In other words, with the *Brown* decision, black parents assumed a position of power that they could use to in effect "force" the School to take on the complete responsibility of educating their children.

With this new power position, the African American parents of my primary case study–the parents we see in the headlines of failing schools of color–have interpreted the *educational contract*, as far as they could tell, in their favor. However, their interpretation has positioned them at a disadvantage in a politics of credibility. Their credibility was undermined because they interpreted their role in their children's educational lives using a value system that is drastically different from what the School uses. The risks of interpretation are high, given that it is fundamental to our co-operative living, and yet it is so subjective. Therefore, in order for speakers and listeners to interpret an utterance (a word, sound, or expression), text, or meaning in the context of radical linguistic and social difference without distortion, Donald Davidson (1984) proposes that there has to be what he calls "the principle of charity." In this principle, speakers and listeners "charitably negotiate" using the rule that the other is acting according to a set of standards that are like their own. This principle is the quintessential missing link between these parents and the School. Therefore, the *extreme* outsourcing of their responsibility of education to the School, to the point of invoking a *sense of entitlement*, has been interpreted by the School, the media, and the country at-large as "irrational." The inevitable demands that this group of parents are making upon the school system through their interpretation of the *educational contract* are being dismissed as "not worth listening to," or as "without credibility" or "without legitimacy." Thus, giving credence to Davidson's notion that if we cannot find a way to interpret the utterances and behaviors of another, then we have no reason to count them "as saying any-thing."(Davidson, 1984)

As a consequence, parents have been rendered irrelevant in the educational outcomes of their children; and this is an ironic paradox given that parental involvement is such a crucial component to academic success of students. Equally consequential, our government has sought and developed other ways for holding schools accountable to the educational achievements of students. Unfortunately, the most effective way we have found to develop this accountability is through numbers–the performance numbers of standardized testing.

As a result, the School determines the acceptability of students with test scores. In other words, using test scores the School determines whether students are authentically learning; but because students are only identified by the numbers they bear on standardized tests, their test scores not only authenticates their learning, but also their very being as "recognized," "acceptable" or "unacceptable." (The terms in quotations are the rankings that a student or school receives based on performance on the standardized tests in Texas.)

Shaped by Language

The test scores become the "legitimate" language–the only language that is understood–to talk about students. Therefore, relationships within the *educational contract* are positioned by the test scores of students. In essence, the utterance (the expression) *"test scores,"* is a linguistical product that mediates a relationship between the School and the various parties in the *educational contract*. For example, within the framework of the linguistic product relation *test scores,* a child is situated in the position of test-taker, "exemplary," "recognized," "unacceptable," "passing," "failing," (words in quotations are taken from the state standardized assessment material and from classroom assessment materials). Adults (not School personnel) are located in the position of responsible parents, irresponsible, negligent, capable, incapable, legitimate or illegitimate. Adults in the classroom assume the position of good teacher or bad teacher (in relation to how well they prepare students to produce high test scores). The *test scores* of the standardized tests take the position of determiner of "recognized," which according to Dictionary.com is to perceive as existing or true (in essence, your test dictates your authenticity) or of "unacceptable," which according to Dictionary.com is to not be capable or worthy of being accepted (in essence, your test dictates your worthiness of being a member of mainstream society).

The utterance *test scores* has become a fundamental tool that is used to mediate an ideological homogenous image of an "American." In essence, in order to be someone that our society "recognizes," (or assumes is relevant and should be considered in policies and laws, and traditions and values) you must look like the quintessential image of an "American"; and that image is shaped by your ability to pass required standardized tests. If you do not have the capability or capacity to pass the standardized test, then you are not really a part of the ideal image of an "American." Antonio Gramsci (1971) argued that the control of creating and maintaining such an ideal could not be sustained for any real length of time without consent of the people through ideological persuasion–or through what he termed "hegemony." Hegemony is the idea of government and nongovernment institutions working together so seamlessly to define an ideal that you cannot tell where one entity ends and another begins. All ideological interests unite and/or fragment in efforts to control national definitions of "acceptable." America, as a nation, has been forged through ideological persuasions.

For instance, news stories about test scores are repeatedly about *test scores* being the sole determiner of the fate of a school. The actual scores are often never even mentioned in the stories, only the result of having the scores as an existence in the system of the school. For instance, two stories randomly taken from the Internet, one from the Houston Chronicle, in Houston TX and the other from the Mercury News in San Jose, CA. show how the existence of the utterance *test scores,* without the numbers it represents, alters the structure of the *contract.*

Sample 1:

Houston Chronicle: Published January 8, 2004 • Zanto Peabody

Fourteen schools cited as failing

Parents of students at fourteen struggling campuses in the Houston area can remove their children from schools that performed poorly on state tests.

Nine schools in the Houston Independent School District can lose students based on their Texas Assessment of Knowledge and Skills test scores. Jones, Houston, Waltrip and Yates high schools made the list. Williams and Ryan middle schools, Grissom and Tinsley elementary and Banneker-McNair Math Academy also reported poor test scores.

Last week, the Texas Education Agency notified academically troubled schools that parents may transfer their children to other campuses. The schools have until Feb. 1 to notify parents of their options.

Sample 2:

Thu, Oct. 14, 2004

Low test scores mean changes for two S.J. schools

GARDNER TEACHERS MUST REAPPLY FOR NEW PROGRAM
By Larry Slonaker
Mercury News

Gardner Elementary does not look like a "failing" school.

It is situated in one of San Jose's poorer neighborhoods, near Interstate 280 and Highway 87. But the school grounds are meticulously clean; the classrooms are orderly and bright. Students seem eager and happy, and every now and then, one stops Principal Millie Arellano to get a hug.

But Gardner is one of two San Jose schools, -- the other is J.W. Fair Middle School--that the state announced Wednesday will face severe consequences because of persistently low test scores. Their situation reflects the statewide trend, with huge numbers of schools finding that improvement benchmarks are extremely difficult to meet.

There is no mention of the actual numbers of the scores in the entire first article. But what is mentioned is that these schools can lose students (translated: money) based *only* on test scores. There is no mention of the condition of the building, availability or lack of resources, qualification of teachers, participation of parents, etc. Furthermore, in the second example, it is *only* test scores that determine that this school is a "failing" school. If test scores did not exist in this scenario, this school would be considered exemplary.

One of the primary difficulties in fixing public education is in measuring the fixes. Indeed, the measurements have gotten in the way of educating. I don't necessarily think that they have to. I am actually a big proponent of national and state testing. I believe one of the most effective consequences of the "No Child Left Behind Act" that required states to develop an objective state-wide measurement was that these exams revealed egregious acts of school administrators graduating students from high school with an elementary school reading capacity. The purpose of having tests in a school system *should* be to tell teachers what their students understand or not; therefore allowing them to re-teach when necessary and move forward when appropriate.

But, the *current* intended purpose of having these scores in the school system is to a have basic definition of what is "normal" or "standard" or "homogenous." "Test scores" is acting as a mediator to achieving homogeneity.

However, given the history of America, to consider homogeneity means we must also consider the larger implications of being colonized by language. For Frantz Fanon, the psychiatrist and de-colonization theorist, to be colonized by language "...means above all to assume a culture" and to assume the consciousness of the colonizer. (Fanon, 1952). To Fanon, who was born in the French colony of Martinique in 1925, to speak the colonizers' (or in the case of the United States, the slave masters') language, means that one has been aggressively persuaded into accepting the collective consciousness of the colonizing culture, which identifies blackness with a deficit in what it means to be human. These values are pervasively and subtly internalized or "epidermalized" into the consciousness of the colonized, therefore creating a necessary disjuncture between one's own consciousness and one's body. Likewise, to apply the homogenous language of *test scores*–which identifies black students as "unacceptable," and by virtue of connection, black parents as well–is to *language* students and their parents as objectionable, offensive, and intolerable. Furthermore, the homogenous process that is engendered by this utterance mediates the transition of test scores from simply measurements, by which students and schools are assessed, to one of the parties of the *educational contract*.

What's more, within that power relation of the *contract,* "test scores" is elevated to the position of "regulator" of the "legitimate" language when talking about education. It becomes the "legitimate" (or official) language that we all use when we talk about whether education is working or not. The "legitimate" language produces utterances (words, statements, expressions) that are not only to be understood or deciphered, but are also to be valued, evaluated, obeyed, and believed (Bourdieu, 1991). Utterances get their value only in their relationship to a market. By "market" I mean a "social market," in which speakers and listeners negotiate understanding. The legitimate language renders all other linguistic processes, and those persons possessing those processes (parents in *The Bottoms*), as illegitimate or without credibility. Nothing with that label can have authority in the market in which it functions.

The utterance "test scores" is authenticated by "standards," which are set by state and national standardized exams. Standards are formulaic, have no regard for individuality of students, and depend heavily on numbers, forms, and form letters. Consequently, the student is represented by numbers and a limited number of forms that are used to talk with parents about how their children are doing in school. According to the principals of Blackshear Elementary, Ryan Middle and Yates High School, most of their parents have no clue what the numbers, forms, and form letters mean for their children. "Few are in the position to say 'break it down,'" said the principal of Blackshear. Most respond with explosive anger or just stare blankly at the principal. In the next chapter, I present some ethnography on this issue.

CHAPTER 2

The School in The Bottoms

Forms and Forms of Talk

The *educational contract* became dysfunctional when parents abdicated their responsibility for their children's performance *in* school *to* the School. The *contract* ceased to function as a productive means for servicing the children for whom it was designed. However, it is important to point out that the dysfunctionality of the *contract* is being reproduced and further developed by the form of language the School uses, which can be found in the form letters produced by the school, and which is structured by the same literacy practice that structures standardized tests.

The literacy practice of the School is a "form of talk" that is premised on a particular way of reasoning. This form of talk is produced and valued in several places through a scaffolding process–a means through which semiotic practices are valued. Scaffolding is a practice of building one possibility with language on top of others already existing and accepted–building on a "history of practice and speaking to a historically conditioned situation," (Bazerman, 1988). The term "scaffolding" comes from the field of building construction. A scaffolding ladder is built one level at a time; the builders stand on the last level built and build the next level, until they reach the height necessary for their work. Through this valuation process the structure of classroom learning, as well as a particular type of speaking, which is associated with certain social groups, have been established. Furthermore, they contribute to the production and reproduction of social relations of sameness and difference.

In this chapter, I present four letters from the School to parents and analyze the letters using parents' responses. I look at how language is used in these social interactions between the School and parents. The letters are chosen based on primary issues that were plaguing my research schools, those being: 1) expectations and translation of expectations; and 2) abdicating and accepting responsibilities. All of the ethnography in this chapter comes from Blackshear Elementary because the principal of this school at the time of this research was the only principal willing to go on record and allow me to shadow him, do formal interviews, and take copies of documentation sent to parents. These letters and analyses aim to show two things: 1) less than five percent of the parents of Blackshear Elementary, at the time of my research, understood the gravity of the letters that go home, and 2) why so few parents understood the severity of these letters.

Letter #1:

Date:

Name:

Address:

City, State, Zip

Dear _____

Your child _____, is suspended on _____ from Blackshear Elementary to return to campus on _____, with parent(s) for the following misconduct and/or violation of the Houston Independent School District rules, polices or regulations.

Level Three Violation Student Code of Conduct

Failure to comply with reasonable request of school personnel.

Failure to follow school/classroom rules.

Chronic and repeated classroom disruptions.

Mandatory Parent Conference Required to Return.

I have considered reasonable alternatives to suspension and determined that suspension is the most appropriate punishment. You and your child must come in for a conference prior to the student's return to classes. **Please come with your child to the conference on March 18 prior to 9:00 am.**

If you have any questions, please call me at (713) xxx –xxxx.

Sincerely,

Principal

To sufficiently read this letter, one would need, at the very least, comprehension capacity at the high school level–a very good high school. Most of the parents of my primary research do not have this capacity level. Therefore, the task of reading these letters alone can be daunting, but also expecting parents to act upon them is unreasonable (unreasonable = irrational, excessive, extreme). Have you ever received an email that said you were part of a class action suit simply because you used a particular service during a particular period? The email goes on with a quite lengthy explanation about the service, the infraction, the suit, and what you need to do if you want to opt out.

What do you do with those emails? File them in case you might want to refer to them later? Trash them? Hope for the best and ignore them? Or do you spend a couple of hours reading them, trying to understand the content? Not many of us take the latter option. The form letters that the School sends home to my research parents are basically like these emails. The content is so mechanical and the language is so unfamiliar that they often just ignore them. They suspect that if there really is a problem, they will get a phone call from the School (or worst, but not uncommon, the police). That's the unfortunate truth.

The tone of the letter is completely sterile–there's no indication of the school having any type of relationship with the child or the family. It reads like an encyclopedia of "standardized" words, which are beyond the reading level of most of the parents. But it is an effective custom for the school to use, because the letter has been approved by the school district's legal department ensuring they are protected from any potential legal repercussions. It is also handy, because so many of these letters are needed during a typical week in schools operating in *The Bottoms*. With these form letters, the school's administrative staff doesn't have to spend limited time sitting down and writing a letter that is unique, and individualized for the child and the specific circumstances of the classroom experience, or that considers the challenges the student and her family may be facing that would cause such behavior.

This abandonment of individualized prescriptive learning is a tragic conundrum for our public education system. Funding for public schools in Texas, and not unlike most states around the U.S., is woefully biased in favor of more affluent neighborhoods.

A state district judge in Austin, TX recently ruled that the funding mechanism that Texas' school system uses is unconstitutional. The bottom fifteen percent of Texas' poorest school districts are taxed an average of $.08 cents more than the wealthiest fifteen percent, but the poorest districts receive about $43,000.00 less per classroom–that's not only unconstitutional; that is a moral tragedy of disproportionate realities. Funding in poor neighborhood schools is extremely limited, which means the administration of those schools are over-whelmed with several jobs. There is little time to focus on the children–children who need an excessive amount of attention because they are already behind in their learning process when they enroll in school; children whose parents pay more for their children's education but get woefully little in return. More than seventy-five percent of the administrator's time is focused on improving test scores.

The irony of those last two realities (administrators have little time to focus on learning, yet spend most of their time trying to improve test scores) is lost in the cracks of trying to create a process for making large school systems function efficiently. If your responsibility is to ensure hundreds of thousands of students are having authentic learning experiences, the most effective way to do that is to have a standardized test that "objectively" determines if students are able to perform certain functions and have certain knowledge by the time they reach a certain grade.

The problem, however, is that while the test is the same, the learning is not. A recent report from the U.S. Office of Civil Rights documented that if students receive math in the lower elementary grades, they perform more than eighty percent better on math in the high school grades. However, the report went on to say that less than forty percent of black and Latino students get math in the lower elementary grades. Furthermore, according to the Education Trust, in the crucial middle school years, sixty-nine percent of fifth-eighth grade students are taught math by teachers who are not certified or have a degree in math! Yet, all students are tested on the same "objective" tests in the high school grades. Objectivity becomes extremely suspect in such scenarios. The nature of "objective" is that it is supposed to be inherently unbiased. It deals in "fact" only; it should not be influenced by opinions or feelings. However, if the objectivity (or the facts) is based in the experience of one group over another group, then the objectivity loses credibility.

Objectivity is what the form letters of this chapter seek to administer, by dealing with things neutrally and impartially rather than with thoughts or feelings, which is more "natural" for people to do. Therefore, the "human" element is deliberately removed from these letters. Yet, the school is confounded when the "human" element in parents that the school expects to provoke with these letters is absent.

This letter went home with a fourth grade student after several attempts to reach the family by phone. Every phone number on record was disconnected, and the boy was not forthcoming with a new one. The next day at 12:30 pm the boy was discovered in the boys' bathroom. He had been there all day. He came to school for breakfast, and slipped into the boys' room. The principal was informed that the boy was at breakfast, and so the principal went searching for him. After finding him in the boys' room, the principal finally got a working number from the boy, and called his mother, who responded with: "I didn't know. Why didn't ya'll call home?" The principal explained the situation: that the boy had "seriously violated school policy, failed to comply with school personnel and was chronically disruptive to the classroom," and that he was being suspended for three days. There was complete silence on the other end. The principal called the parent's name and asked if she was still there. She said, "Yes," and they ended the conversation.

The next day, it's thirty-five degrees outside, and the boy is seen again in the cafeteria eating breakfast, and it was reported to the principal. The principal went looking for the boy in his classroom; the teacher had not seen him. The principal looked in the bathroom, the boy was not there.

The principal called home:

Principal: "Ms. Jones," where is your son?
Mother: I think the daycare bus brought him to school.
Principal: Remember our conversation yesterday?
Mother: Oh yeah. He's suspended.
Principal: Well, he's missing.
Mother: Don't worry, the daycare bus picks him up at 3:00. He'll probably be back in time for the daycare bus.

The principal didn't wait. He called the police, but they were not able to find the boy. At 2:50 pm the child showed up at the school. The principal, visibly upset, asked the child: "Where have you been all day?" The principal's annoyance with the situation came to a sudden halt when the boy answered: "It was cold out here today." The boy figured if he hid in the bathroom he would be found, so he had been sitting on the porch of some random house where no one was home. He sat there, outside all day, from 7:40 in the morning until 2:50 in the afternoon, in the cold.

In a formal interview with the principal about the letters sent to parents:

Principal: They don't get it and will never get it. There is a breakdown between procedure and the impact of that procedure. The idea is that a procedure, such as a child being suspended twice, will have an impact. Hopefully the institutional response [suspension] would get a personal response. But you see nothing changed.

Researcher: Why is that?

Principal: The school communicates with parents in a politicized legalized language, for example a language of expectations. A parent may not understand "expectation" and may not be in the position to say: "What is expectation?" For example, the language of the school is: "Nobody's child is bad; children make poor choices, and your child might need an alternative learning environment" vs. "Your kid's an asshole and he's going to have to go to Alternative School." Now that they'd understand. But it's also very likely that it would degenerate into physical violence. We have to elevate our language to a level of high expectations and be careful not to descend to using violent words or physical violence as a first resort. And for children who don't communicate with their parents, it could be an unreasonable expectation to ask them to respect adults.

The principal's comments show that it is not the word "expectations" that parents or children are not getting, but rather the School's ideology of the word. Parents and students are expected to behave in a certain way based on an action of the School, an action that is situated in the School's idea of "parent behavior," "student behavior," or "parent-child" behavior. However, the School has not engaged the parent in this process as an individual person, with unique experiences and therefore distinctive understandings. The School has engaged the parent as a metaphorical "standardized form letter." There is nothing in these letters that suggests that the School even knows who the child really is, and certainly does not hint at any knowledge of the parent. The parent becomes a "standard procedure." She is simply a "course of action" that must be taken, but not really engaged with from a human perspective.

Letter #2

Dear Parents,

On Tuesday, it was brought to my attention that one of our students had written a list that was titled "Hit List" that included the names of several classmates.

Evidence was presented to me and, after my investigation, administrative action was taken in regards to the author of the list in accordance with the HISD Code of Student Conduct. HISD Police was contacted and an investigation was opened to determine an appropriate course of action beyond my administrative action already taken. Consequences were assigned to the author of the list and we are cooperating with law enforcement officials to complete the gathering evidence to ensure a thorough presentation of facts to all agencies involved.

Measures were taken to ensure that no weapons were present on campus and no explicit plans were expressed in terms of committing actual harm to any students.

In light of HISD's Core Value of Safety Above All Else, we are acting to ensure a safe learning environment for all of our students and we take situations such as this very seriously. I am truly grateful for and commend the work of our HISD Police Department, the South Central District Office, HISD Administration and our community for the support and cooperation in providing our students with the best possible chance to achieve success in a safe school.

I would ask you to take this opportunity to discuss with your children the seriousness of any type of threatening, physical, written or verbal communication, as we will consistently respond quickly and to the full extent of the law in matters of student safety.

If you would like to discuss this issue further, please do not hesitate to visit me at the school or to contact me at 713-xxx-xxxx.

Principal: What's missing from that letter?

Researcher: What was actually done.

Principal: Exactly. It's not in there...eighty-five percent of parents who got the letter have no idea what it says. Only five [out of 437] parents questioned it. And I told them, "We assessed the consequences as according to the Code of Conduct."

Researcher: What does that mean?

Principal: Exactly. But no one asked me that.

Situations like the one in this letter are not that uncommon in the type of schools where I work. However, because the behavior has "crossed over" to schools in more affluent Anglo neighborhoods, it has recently become an "epidemic." We are currently talking a lot about gun control in the country (in 2013) because of the recent tragedy in Newtown CN, where twenty elementary school children and six adults were killed in their school. The week before that event, the exact same number (twenty-six) of young people had been killed on the streets of Chicago over a weekend. There was no media or political outcry, because the occurrence is so frequent. Because violence is so pervasive in my research schools, and similarly situated schools and communities across the country, parental response is often as it was in the case of Letter #2.

The families of my primary research use violence to manage their lives. I talk more about how such a way of living came to be in Chapter 3. If we do not wake up and pay attention to what is going on in our urban centers, the problem will be of astronomical proportions for all of us. First of all, the problem has already begun to spill over into the suburbs; and it will become more pervasive. Secondly, most of our population is condensed in large inner-city areas, which means most of our intellectual and economic human resources are also in the same areas. If we continue to allow that population to deteriorate, then so will our country. Our economy will suffer, because there will be too few people qualified to participate in the increasingly advanced technologically required labor force, and too few to buy our products or pay taxes. We will not only be importing our goods from China, but also our talent. As a matter of fact, the number of teachers that we currently import for math and science from Asian countries has increased by more than thirty percent over the years.

Letter #3:

TO: The Parents of
FROM: Mr. Reed, Principal
RE: Gang Activity
DATE: April 16, 2004

Dear Parent,

This letter is to inform you that your child has been identified as a participant in gang activity at PS Elementary School. After counseling with the Principal and a member of the Police Department's Gang Task Force, your child was made aware that any future violations of the Code of Student Conduct that involved three or more of this group would be considered gang activity and would be subject to citation and a court appearance.

In the event that further disruptions or violations occur, your child will be subject to disciplinary policies as delineated in the Code of Student Conduct, including suspension and/or placement in a District Alternative Educational Program.

A copy of this letter is being forwarded to the Police Department and will be used as evidence if this behavior persists.

I look forward to meeting with you in regards to this matter.

This letter went out to ten parents; none of them questioned the process of police interrogating a minor without having a parent present. One parent called the principal:

Mother: Does this mean my son is going to jail?

Principal: A copy of this letter has been forwarded to the police.

Mother: Are you kicking him out a school?

Principal: If he continues to violate the Code of Conduct, there will be an investigation.

Mother: I don't' understand.

Principal: Right now, he's here, and if he stays out of trouble, he will stay here.

Mother: But if he don't, where do he go?

Principal: He will receive a citation and will have to appear in court.

Mother: You mean a real court or a school court.

Principal: He will have to appear in a criminal court.

Mother: I don't understand. Is that a real court?

Principal: Yes, that is a real court.

Mother: Dis don't make no fuckin sense.

This conversation went on for over an hour, before the parent could understand a 144 word letter.

These first three letters highlight one of the primary reasons so few parents are responding: The letters are just almost completely incomprehensible to them. Yet, these letters are about their children, so why are parents not more aggressive with obtaining clarification? With Letter #4, I show why parents are so easily dissuaded by the form of talk the school uses. Parents are essentially rendered irrelevant.

Letter #4:

Parent Notification of Student Performance
Texas Assessment of Knowledge & Skills Test
February 2005 Administration

DID NOT MEET STANDARD
March 15, 2005

Dear Parents:

During February 2005, your student, _____,
was given the Texas Assessment of Knowledge and Skills
(TAKS) in reading. The results of your student's test are
attached along with a brochure, "Understanding the
Confidential Student Report," developed by the Texas
Education Agency to help you understand your child's test
results.

Your child:
   -Did not meet the standard on the Reading test.
   -Was absent/did not receive a score.

Under Texas law, your student must meet the state standard
on the Reading test in order to be promoted. If your student

did not pass the Reading section of this test, the next test administration will be April 20 (Wednesday) Reading.

The School will provide your student with the following intervention services in order to gain the knowledge and skills necessary for successful performance on the test(s):

√ Summer School TAKS Intervention Class

√ After school TAKS Intervention Class

√ Tutorial Pull-outs

√ Reading Intervention Coach/Master Reading Teacher

The campus will be closely monitoring your student's progress. You are encouraged to contact the school to learn more about how you can help your student gain the necessary knowledge and skills to pass the state's TAKS Exit Level assessment.

Sincerely,

Principal

_____

This letter was sent to sixty-eight percent of Blackshear Elementary School parents on a Wednesday; by the following Friday, not one parent had called in or come to the school to inquire further about this letter.

The week following that Friday was Spring Break, when no one would be at the School. When they returned to school, teachers would have only one week to work with students to prepare them to "meet the standard" in a second testing. However at the bottom of this letter in bold and italics, is this note to parents: "You are *encouraged* to contact the school" (my emphasis in italics). There is no level of what the parent *must* do, as there is for the student, who "**must** meet the state standard on the Reading test." Parents are relieved of their responsibility of having to meet any expected standard in two ways: 1) They were only *encouraged* to contact the school; and 2) They were not given any information specific to their children's weaknesses, nor were they given any academic material they could use to help their children during the week there was no school, only two weeks before the children re-tested.

In addition, this letter, which is written to parents, describes the child as "your student." In this letter the child's identity is determined by his role in the school, even at home, outside the school. The role "student" trumps the role "child." This definition of the child serves to further separate the parent from responsibility of what goes on with the child with regard to education.

You might be thinking, parents should be the primary teacher for their children, and I agree. But the term "student" is assigned to the domain of "School." By saying to the parent "your student," it diminishes the intimacy of the parent-child power relation; and thereby diminishes the responsibility of parents on the matter of education.

This form letter is *the* letter that was used throughout this District, at the time of this research, to inform parents of student progress. Based on this letter, it would seem that the School has decided that parents either do not need individual and curricular information to assist the School in preparing the child, or that parents would not use such information. In any event, the School has assumed the role of being solely accountable for student achievement. Therefore, it becomes easy for parents to assume a position of irrelevance. There is no accountability for parents.

The principal at Blackshear elementary school gave this speech to his fifth graders on the day the first test results came in:

This is the state of Texas [he held up a copy of the state reading test]. Seventeen people passed, that's two out of three people failed! They don't care about love, they don't care about compassion, they don't care about how hard it is for you at home. There are thirty multiple choice questions. Did you do it? Yes or No. That's it, either 'Yes' you met the standard, or 'No' you did not. That's all they care about. You invited 'No' into your life. We have three days to turn No into Yes. On April 20, you get a second chance. Do not let the fifth grade be the most important two, three, or four years of your life.

Students were "graded" on standardized tests with the terms "Yes" and "No," meaning "Yes" they met the standard, or "No" they did not meet the standard. Whether they met the standard was determined by the number of questions answered correctly on the test–at least twenty-nine correctly answered questions out of thirty-five was required to meet the standard. In Chapter 4, I talk more about the symbolism of this notion of a "standard." The principal's lecture took a slight turn as he began to plead for himself, the school, the students, and the community.

Douglass is closing down. (Douglass is another elementary school that the District closed because of low performance and low attendance). You gotta help me. Help this community. Help yourself. I have dreams to make this a great school, but I can't do it without you. You are dis-servicing yourself. We have three days to get it right. This [a public education] is the last free thing you're gonna get.

The principal's pleas to the humanity of students, was a grasping for straws. Even if he were able to penetrate the child's sense of compassion to help him, the school and the community, it would do them no good, as he himself exclaimed, on these tests. They would either meet the standard or they would not. There is only one correct answer and the tests are graded by a machine. There is no way to grade the students' compassion for the principal or their community on these tests. However, the principal seemed to be suggesting that the students' compassion would be determined by them passing this test. This would then suggest a "natural" link between their intellectual capability and their moral way of being.

There were no such meetings or pleas, however, with parents. If such a meeting had been held with parents, the school could have demonstrated with more compelling urgency the importance of these exams; and the school could have held workshops for parents to learn how to help their children over the break. Nevertheless, only a form letter that was entrusted with third and fifth grade students (roughly, age eight to eleven) was sent home. Because of a lack of human and financial resources to carry out a large mass mailing in a short time, the letter was not mailed, which means most parents didn't even get the notification. If you're a parent or have ever been a student entrusted with taking home letters from your elementary school, then you know it's a gamble how many of those papers actually get to parents. Teachers were told to make follow-up phone calls, but the administration could not enforce this directive because teachers would have had to carry it out on their "own time." They only had three days before they would go on Spring Break, and the prospect of calling the homes of thirty or more children and restructuring their entire curricula to get these children ready to retest, seemed to be, on the principal's part, "struggling hopefulness" at best.

In a formal interview, the principal told me this: "We are dealing with human beings. And there is no room for that in this assessment tool, or in the way schools are run... School has been turned into multiple choice circles." And like the form letters that make little

to no sense to the parents, the multiple choices presented on standardized exams make little to no sense to the
children. For example, the skill of inferring is a key skill
in every section of the Texas state test. To infer is to
arrive at a conclusion by reasoning from explicit, and
equally important, implicit evidence that is presented.
A sample third grade question: Mr. Lewis is wearing
brown shoes, Ms. Perry is wearing white shoes, Mr.
Jackson is wearing blue shoes, and Ms. Jones is not
wearing black shoes or the same color shoes as the
others. What color are Ms. Jones' shoes? The choices
are: A) Brown; B) Blue; C) White; D) Black; E) Pink.

The child is supposed to infer that Ms. Jones is
wearing pink shoes, even though the word "pink" is not
mentioned in the text of the question. The form letters
that the School uses to communicate with parents also
assume that parents will take meaning in the same way
that standardized exams assume the child will take
meaning. Both objects–the exams and the form letters–
assume a particular form of reasoning is at work.

CHAPTER 3

The Families in The Bottoms

The School assumes parents living in *The Bottoms* are processing information about their children's needs similarly to the way the School does. The school assumes that parents are making decisions by manipulating language. In other words, they assume that if parents get a letter from the school about their children's educational needs, then parents will be able to weigh the gravity of the consequences simply based on reading the letter. The School also assumes that parents have the same values, beliefs and traditions and that these practices will provoke the response the School wants to get from parents. However, for this group of families, drawing conclusions from information presented to them is not processed with the same values (the same level of importance) or the same reasoning process (through the manipulation of language). Making decisions is usually done through lived experiences that are counted as mistakes, rather than through the manipulation of language. For example, seventeen-year-old Kenny Freeman, whose family lives in *The Bottoms* and represents the families of my primary case study, told this story:

One day when I didn't pick up these bricks that was in the front yard. I guess my grandpa was drunk or mad, something. But he woke me up by slappin me across the head, and when I woke up he was asking me why haven't I pick up those two big bricks with the hole in them. I guess I gave him the wrong answer because he hit me again, twice this time...

Reasoning

You see, Kenny reasoned that he must have given the wrong answer, BECAUSE his grandfather HIT him ("twice this time"). Kenny did not make his conclusion through a verbal exchange of words (or manipulating language) with his grandfather. This reasoning process is a product of Kenny's rearing, therefore a part of the values, beliefs and traditions of his family. It is structured by the need to experience the consequences of choices before they can realize that the choice was a good one or not. What's more, determining whether a choice was good or not is linked to physical pain or the threat of it.

There's something very curious about this notion of a sequential thought process for taking meaning from events being inextricably linked to violence. Manipulating language to make a choice or determine if the choice might be good is not something that these families have been taught to do. Consequently, children perform poorly in school. At the time of this research, seventy percent of the students of Blackshear Elementary, the zoned (or assigned) elementary school for *The Bottoms*, failed to meet the standards for passing the Texas Assessment of Knowledge and Skills reading exams (the official State test at that time). At the zoned middle school, Ryan Middle, sixty-five percent failed, and at the zoned high school, Jack Yates High, sixty-eight percent failed.

The percentage of children failing these literacy exams, which correlated with the number of students failing school, also correlated to the percentage of parents whose involvement with their children's school life was extremely low. By "school life" I mean, they did not help their children prepare to be successful in school. These were the same parents who did not read bedtime stories to their children before bed (which builds literacy skills); or teach them the alphabet or numbers or shapes or colors before enrolling them into school.

However, as I've mentioned in earlier chapters, for the most part, this practice is not a tradition of willful neglect; it is a custom with deep historical roots in what is *known* to these parents, who learned their literacy practices from their parents, who learned their literacy practices from their parents, and so on... The children of *The Bottoms* follow paths of development in literacy orientations that are drastically different from what we find in School. We can see how these educational orientations were developed by looking at what goes on in story-reading and other literacy-related interactions between adults and preschoolers at home.

The Bottoms

The Bottoms, a black working-poor-class community, is encircled by: Downtown Houston, which over the past decade has become a very expensive place to live; the University of Houston, which has become a Tier One university; and Texas Southern University, an historic black college with a legacy that extends back to the emancipation from slavery. *The Bottoms* is known by this name, because it is literally at the bottom of the list for all social services (at the time of this research). The blacktop roads that run through the community are bounded on both sides by very deep trenches to catch rain water so that the neighborhood doesn't flood during tropical rain storms that are known as regular occurrences in Houston. The roads are extremely narrow, so rain water isn't the only thing the trenches catch–people often back their cars up too far when pulling out of their driveways and fall into the trenches.

It is a literate community in the sense that the residents are able to read printed and written materials in their daily lives, and they produce written messages as part of the total pattern of communication in the community. Children go to school with the expectation of encountering print materials, and children have an understanding that reading is something one does to learn something one needs to know.

In *The Bottoms* (at the time of this research) most infants would come home from the hospital to what I am describing as an entirely adult environment. There were no specific objects for the baby—no cribs, no toys or mobiles, or car seats (despite the law that dictated that infants should be strapped in a car seat). In most cases, the mother had the consciousness to sit in the back seat of the car to protect her baby, but the child comes home, exposed to a physically vulnerable situation, already at risk and without the "normal" things that would support her survival.

It was not unusual for infants to sleep in bed with parents until about two years old. They ate and slept in the midst of human talk and noise from the television, stereo and radio. They were encapsulated in an almost totally adult world in the midst of constant adult communications, verbal and nonverbal. As a consequence, they become particularly sensitive to the movements of those who hold them (which later proved to be a critical link in how they learn—building a "bond" with their teacher is crucial). When the child can crawl, she plays with the household objects deemed safe (plastic dishes, spoons, etc.). In most instances, only at Christmas and birthdays are there "special toys"–which are usually the latest trending hip hop clothes and sneaker fashions, sports gear, dolls, or technological gadgets that have a pension toward violence; but rarely manipulative toys, like blocks, puzzles, or take-apart toys or literacy based items, such as letter games or books. In most all cases, there are no reading materials for children. Preschoolers are not read to by adults. And since children are usually left to sleep whenever and wherever they fall asleep, there was no bedtime or naptime as such. Going to bed was not framed in any special routine, such as a bedtime story, which serves to predispose children to a practice that is akin to class-room learning–and which serves as a foundation for establishing the literacy skills that are necessary to be successful in classroom learning and on standardized tests.

When children uttered sounds or combinations of sounds, no attention was given to the sound or the child. Babbling sounds (the early stage of language develop-ment) were referred to as "noise" and no effort was made to acknowledge and interpret these sounds as words or a means of communication.

At about two years old children began to imitate complete utterances they heard around them, which were typically not in the form of standard English. Therefore, when they arrived to school on their very first day, they were already two to four years behind the curve in learning language.

At three years old they began to mimic what they saw on television, which was disproportionately slanted toward violent acts against others (especially women) and music-based TV shows. Although children did watch animated children's shows, they were generally shows that included conflict and fighting (i.e. Ninja Turtles, super heroes battling an evil enemy). As a result, it was not uncommon to see children using their hand to create the image of a gun, while pointing it at each other or even at cartoon characters in television shows.

Between three and four years old, children took part in creatively complex movement patterns of dance and learn the lyrics to entire songs—lots of songs. They also seemingly intuitively learned the rhythmic flow of these songs; and that flow permeated the flow of other activities. For example, the way they approached learning was to do so in a pace that was reminiscent of the pattern of the kind of music they listened to. If the music was rap music, their attention span was significantly shorter than if the music was R&B. If they listened mostly to gospel music, they had a tendency to express more hopefulness in their ability to accomplish tasks and there was more patience for reaching their goals. From the time they were old enough to stand alone, they were encouraged to participate in exercises that built their intelligence for kinesthetic skills, practices, and knowledge.

The result in school is that these children start school with skills that are highly recognized outside of school–skills that are recognized in sports, arts, and performance programs. They are very adept at kinesthetic and artistic endeavors that require a rhythmic use of their body (such as sports, dance, and music), expressions of color (such as drawing and painting) and creative word play (such as found in hip hop poetry). However, except for official high school boys' football or basketball teams, these classes have been stripped from their schools in favor of print-based test preparation methodologies, such as worksheets.

As preschoolers, they did not learn skills that are valued in academia and emphasized in the early grades, such as learning to label, list features and give what Shirley Brice Heath calls "what-explanations" to "what-questions" such as *What's that? Who's that*? For example, if a teacher asks, "what color is x?" Instead of naming or identifying the color, the child might respond with, "It is the color of my mama's favorite car that she wants to get with her income tax money..." The answers are rich in context, but not likely to appear as an option on a standardized test or a multiple choice test (such as blue, green, red). So, when faced with choices that do not make sense–and having no way of expressing or even recognizing the source of their confusion–the student is stumped.

Furthermore, their reasoning process (the process for how these children and their families arrive at reasoning) is shaped by violence and an abdication of one's responsibility through hundreds of seemingly mundane activities, such as a mother diapering her baby.

When mother is diapering baby, mother generally makes eye contact with baby to keep baby calm, however mother is simultaneously in conversation with another adult about a subject that has nothing to do with baby or with diapering baby. If baby is crying, mother expresses her own frustration with baby's behavior, in an aggressive manner, sparking a set of actions that depend on how baby behaves. For instance, if baby cries louder, mother raises her voice to be louder than baby's. If baby continues to cry, mother starts to use violent language. If anyone challenges mother for her behavior, she blames baby for "making" her lose her temper. At no time is baby's frustration with the diapering attended to or acknowledged–or "given voice"; nor does mother take any responsibility for her own behavior.

Another example: children are instructed to complete household tasks, but there is no effort to teach children how to do these things and there are no established routines. The practice is sporadic and usually demanded by the adults out of a moment of frustration. No guidance on how to perform tasks or why they are necessary is given. If children ask questions about the task, it may be considered "talking back" or disrespectful, and they are told to "just do it" or "figure it out." So they are silenced, resulting in missing a valuable opportunity to experience a "teachable moment" to learn important life skills, character development, positive habits, but most important to this research, academic skills that prep them for how classroom learning occurs.

As a consequence, children do not have conversations with adults. In conversation, speakers negotiate meaning and interpretation through the manipulation of language. For example, if your mother told you to clean your room, but you didn't do it, then in conversation, your mother might learn that you thought you had done it; therefore the problem is that you didn't know what a clean room looks like. But, if there is no conversation, your mother might think you simply disobeyed her and might respond with a spanking or with violent language, leaving you to figure out on your own what went wrong.

In conversation there is the opportunity for both parties to express their thoughts, consider new ways of thinking, explore new outcomes. The children of *The Bottoms* do not learn these techniques in the formative years of their educational development. Therefore, in text exercises they are faced with the unfamiliar process of manipulating language to come to a decision. Furthermore, they do not learn that there is a process to how things are accomplished; for them, there are no steps to get from Point A to Point D. What's more, children learn to react to events, with the understanding that their action was a response to something done to them—not something for which they share responsibility. As a result, when social situations become disagreeable, the students and their parents are unable to see their part in the breakdown and they lack the skills to come to an understanding. This same dynamic transpires in the relationship between parent and teacher and administrators. Thus you have parents responding belligerently to the expectations of the School. For example, a parent met with the elementary school principal after she received a letter that her child was going to be suspended for the third time in November 2004. At the time of this research, the illustration of this behavior represented approximately one-third of the parenting situations at Blackshear Elementary:

Principal: Joe's behavior is so disruptive that he is failing all of his classes and state tests. He is also making it next to impossible for other students to focus on work.

Mother: [She says with all sincerity] I didn't know this was going on.

Principal: Didn't you know that he had been suspended twice before?

Mother: Uh. I don't remember.

Principal: Have you seen his report card?

Mother: He hasn't brought one home?

Principal: It's November, four months in the school year and you haven't suspected that he might have at least one report card yet?

Mother is silent, but is clearly getting angry, as the principal is attempting to get her to take some responsibility in this matter.

Principal: What are we going to do about this?

Mother: Is my son's teacher a man or a woman; cause he ain't gone listen to no woman. You need to put him in a man's class.

The principal of Blackshear Elementary claims this type of behavior is a product of eroded morals and an elasticity of consequences and expectations on the part of parents. However, given the history of black peoples in this country, I encourage you to consider that there is more going on than just simply relinquishing one's responsibility and feeling entitled.

As I explained more fully in Chapter 1, there is a historically conditioned pattern at work that precipitated this group's interpretation of the *Brown* case. Although it is in complete dissimilarity to the intended outcome of the case, their understanding of their role in the educational lives of their children is only this: send the kid to school.

Therefore, I am led to consider that what seems to be a lack of parent participation in urban public schools of color is actually quite the opposite–parents are fully participating in their understanding of the *educational contract*. Furthermore, I am suggesting that the behavior of these parents of this *contract* is intertwined with the structure of the *contract*. Parents of large urban public schools of color have gone through a socialization process and have become dependent on this existing social structure. By that I mean, while on one side there are situated actors who undertake social action and interaction (human agency); on the other side, and at the same time, there are also the rules, resources, and social relationships that are produced and reproduced in social interaction (structures). Parents have agreed that the School should be responsible for educating their children. And parents have become dependent upon that knowledge–they have left that job to the School.

In response to the parent's way of participating, the School's expectations have shifted. It is no longer accountable to parents, but now to test scores; and it no longer depends on parents' help, but heavily depends on students.

Blackshear Elementary principal said:

We want students to take ownership of the results of test scores. [For example] If I can't read r-o-c-k-s, I have a choice–determine the value of reading it and practice it; or not. It has to be important to me [as a student] to pass to the sixth grade, whatever else is going on my life, whatever else happens, this has to be most important. That's a lot to ask from a nine- or ten-year-old.

It is also a lot to ask of a sixteen or seventeen-year-old because there are so many other things that seem to take precedence over school.

Kenny:

I used to dream about my mother every night, most of them I dream that she was dead or somebody killed her in front of me. And every time I wake up I thought she was dead for real cause I never seen her. And if I did, she will come to grandma house, and see me for about five minutes and disappear like a I wasn't her child. I just didn't know my mother that well until I turn around fourteen years old. I also didn't have a father, or didn't even know my father, and right now today I still don't know my father. That's why I want to be home for my son.

To ask a child to put off the more pressing matters of being hungry or watching his mother destroy herself with crack cocaine on a back burner and just focus on passing his state standardized test is a stretch at best. Kenny was in boot camp as I began to wrap up this research. Boot camp is for youth criminal offenders under the age of eighteen, but for all intents and purposes, it is jail. This was his second time going to boot camp. He broke into a community center and stole some office equipment. Kenny's mother has been addicted to crack cocaine since before his birth. His father is in prison. His grandparents raised him from infancy. His grandfather (who we met at the beginning of this chapter), who sincerely loved Kenny and his two siblings but had a strange way of demonstrating it, recently died. His grandmother was exhausted by years of disillusionment and disappointment.

One recent Sunday, "Minnie," Kenny's mom, who was still addicted to crack at the time of this research, came into the church where her children had first gone four years earlier. The children came with such passion that they convinced their grandparents (their caregivers) to come and join the church. Minnie came into this particular Sunday service quite late. The service was nearly over. She stood in the back of the building weeping like a baby. The devastation of crack cocaine to areas in the inner-cities like *The Bottoms* is immense.

Language...again

So how can Kenny's life, and the lives of similar young people who are failing school, be "translated" for the School in order to serve the children more effectively? Like Wittgenstein (1953), I understand language to be the mark of human sociality. And so without a sufficient language we cannot even communicate the problem. That is not to say that it is incommunicable. Only that it is incommunicable in the language in which the decision makers operate. That language being of a bureaucratic nature–forms, form letters, test scores, attendance ratings, and political labels inspired by test scores, such as *at-risk*, *inner-city*, *special education*, *incapable, Recognized, Unacceptable*. This language is, unfortunately for parents, the "legitimate" (or official) language the School uses to talk about students. Parents who live in *The Bottoms* are faced with having to interact with the School in a language that they are not fluent in. Consequently, the *educational contract* and the parents' interpretation are part of a cultural pattern of failure that, in this specific milieu, is being mediated by language. In this pattern of failure, these families are left without a future in this language–they are considered as insignificant to the School's ability to move forward.

Wittgenstein argues in *Philosophical Investigations* that to have a future in language, the child should be enabled to say "and after I had trained my mouth to form these signs, I used them to express my own desires" (Wittgenstein, 1953). Wittgenstein presents a child that moves invisibly among adults, watching them and grasping the signs that represent various objects; and the child training himself to form these signs and then to use them to make expressions. In the "legitimate" (or official) language of the classroom—the language enabled by the standardized exams and by the form letters used by the School—if the student is not able to train herself to form and grasp the use of these signs, she is labeled as "learning disabled," "at-risk," or "a behavioral problem," and therefore rendered without a future in language, and by virtue of connection, so are her parents.

Without a future in language, these families become victims to words being controlled by the ideology they speak. The language that is available to these families—the language of school and district forms and academic standards—makes it next to impossible for these families to communicate effectively with the School, and vice versa. Therefore, the families become "casualties" of the labels that are attached to them.

These labels (*recognized, unacceptable, at-risk, learning disabled*) reflect the thoughts, purposes, and observations of a reality that is expressed in the standards of standardized exams—their literacy practices and form of talk. The exams reflect the thoughts, purposes, and observations of a "perceived social standard," which is an "ideal" by which all "realities" are measured.

CHAPTER 4

The Standard Embodied

Two Comparative Cases

A standard is something considered as a basis for comparison. It is an "approved" model put forth by an authority and propagated by the society as the "norm." It is the "ideal." However, when the standard is made flesh–or when it is embodied in people, for example–it no longer functions as an ideal because of the unstable nature of constantly changing cultural ideas, but rather it functions like the highway mile markers on the road, marking off how far or close you are to a particular destination–in this case, the ideal. My comparative cases, the Strivers and the Manns, represent what the standard looks like when embodied in people. The Mann family is closer to the original ideal of the American family; however, the Strivers have managed to reshape the cultural idea of the standard in order to reflect an embodied standard image.

The Strivers

Angela and Peter Strivers, an upper middle-class black couple, are the parents of Peter Jr., who was a student at Lanier Middle School. His zoned school was Ryan Middle School. They live in the section of Third Ward, that I am calling *Texas Southern University Neighborhood (TSU Neighborhood).* Many of the houses in this area were built during a time of the impeccable craftsmanship of austere two-story brick duplexes. The area was established by former slaves immediately following the emancipation from slavery. The college that sits in the center of the community, Texas Southern University, is one of the oldest black colleges in the nation. Also in the community is the home of the oldest black radio station in the nation. Therefore the neighborhood is steeped in a rich African American history of self-sufficiency, possibilities, and successes. It represents the potentialities available to young black people, who have significantly more resources today than the original residents had when they established a tradition of profound historical acumen.

The boundaries of this neighborhood begin one street south of The Bottoms; yet the residents of TSU Neighborhood are a world away. The zoned schools in TSU Neighborhood are the same schools zoned for *The Bottoms*. Therefore, because most of the people who live in this neighborhood today are upper middle-class black professionals, they drive their children to high performing schools in predominantly white communities.

The Manns

Becky and Bob Mann, an upper middle-class white couple, work at the University of Houston, and their daughter, Joyce, attends one of the exclusive University charter schools. By "exclusive," I mean the schools' populations are small; therefore admission into the schools is highly competitive. The University is in Third Ward, one street to the west of *The Bottoms*, in an area that I will call *The Bayou*.

The bayou is a main waterway that flows approximately fifty-three miles through Houston and then into

Galveston Bay and the Gulf of Mexico. The community that sits along the banks of *The Bayou* near the University of Houston today is an affluent upper middle-class Anglo community. However, this demographic make-up is rather new. At the start of this research, most of the homes in this neighborhood were owned by African Americans. Many of the homes sat empty and boarded up. With the gentrification of downtown Houston, which is only about four miles away, Anglos began buying up the boarded up properties for pennies on the dollar. The neighborhood has gone through almost a complete transition in less than ten years. It is now made up of several exclusive public elementary and middle schools that are connected to the University of Houston.

Mainstream School-Oriented Homes

The Strivers and the Mann families represent the other two communities of parents that have converged in the Third Ward of Houston along with the community of families in *The Bottoms*. The Strivers in *TSU Neighborhood* and the Mann family in *The Bayou* have similarly situated literacy experiences and can be categorized as mainstream school-oriented homes. The children of these two communities of families come home from the hospital to rooms that are decorated with bookcases, murals, bedspreads, mobiles, and stuffed animals which represent characters found in books that are on their book shelves. Because adults always read bedtime stories to children, from an early age, children give attention to books and information printed within them.

Babbling sounds and non-verbal responses made by children are expanded by adults into fully formed grammatical sentences. Furthermore, from this early age, adults not only ask simple questions, "what-explanation" questions (*What's that? Who's that?*), they even extend their questions to ask about the attributes of these items–"reason-explanation" questions (*What shape is the ball? Why is it shaped that way?*).

From the time children start to talk, they respond to conversations that allude to the content of books: they act as thinking beings who have knowledge of the content of books. (i.e. "a furry brown dog on the street" is likened by an adult to "Lassie" in a child's book: "Look, there's Lassie. Do you think he's looking for a boy?'"). Adults model the extension of familiar objects and events from books to new and unfamiliar situations, by: 1) maintaining a running commentary on any event or object which can be book-related; and 2) by taking turns playing labeling games. Beyond two years of age, children begin to make use of what they have come understand about how books tell stories. They announce their own with formulaic openings and conclusions, such as "once upon a time" or "the end." By the time children reach three years old, they learn to listen and wait as an audience, as their parents begin to discourage the highly interactive role they're used to in exchange for teaching them to listen, store what they hear, and on cue from the adult, answer a question–they are ready for how the classroom functions.

Furthermore, in these two communities, story reading sets the stage for a long chain of interrelated literacy practices that help children create meaning in both their academic and non-academic experiences. The patterns begin with children labeling objects and asking what-questions, and this type of knowledge construction process continues into the school experience, making use of running commentaries on old knowledge as they compare it to new knowledge. As I pointed out in the previous chapter, this process is known as "scaffolding" and it characterizes the structure of classroom learning and standardized tests.

The scaffolding process is further reinforced by the daily routines adults have with children, which establish patterns of behavior that serve to further support classroom learning. Consequently, children do very well throughout their academic careers. The routines include playing with manipulative toys like blocks, letters, and numbers; taking on the roles of characters in books, acting out the stories; and verbalizing seemingly mundane activities such as diapering baby. Activities like the latter one actually set the stage for the others to make sense to the child and to prepare the child for school. For example, when diapering baby, mother says, "I'm going to change your diaper," "You help me when you hold still," "Here is your wet diaper," "I'm throwing your wet diaper into the trash," "Here is your new diaper," "It's a dry diaper," "Isn't that much better?" "Yes it is." Any babbling sounds and/or crying baby makes, mother turns into words (giving baby "voice"). For example, if baby is crying, mother might say: "I know you're irritated; it's OK."

This process of engaging baby, first of all, involves mother pointing out what she is doing, step-by-step.

From this activity, baby learns to analyze processes in a step-by-step formation. Things are not just done, but there is a process to them being done. Secondly, mother puts words to what she is doing, and baby begins to associate words with objects. Thirdly, mother speaks in fully formed standard language sentences, which teaches baby to do the same. Fourth, mother assigns words to sounds that baby makes, who learns to associate the words to the sound or the feeling that inspires the sound. Fifth, mother transfers a value judgment when she asks baby, "Isn't that much better?" And she answers, "Yes, it is." She further validates the value of baby's feelings when she says, "I know you're irritated; it's OK."

The same process occurs with all sorts of seemingly ordinary activities, setting a stage for problem solving, and for value laden ideas. This type of interaction provides baby with a foundation to understand how one gets from Point A to Point D. In which case, one can use this understanding to manipulate between the various points and answer, as well as pose, questions from various positions.

Case in point, in story-reading, mother and baby take turns in a dialogue in which the mother directs the baby's attention to a book and labels items on the page and asks a series of questions. The child's reasoning skills are developed as he learns from these exercises that the items on the page are two-dimensional and not like their "real" counterparts–they cannot be grasped and manipulated. Mother compares these items in books to their real counterparts, which helps the child maneuver from Point A (picture of dog in a book) to Point D (his pet dog), and he assigns an independent status to pictures. The child's reasoning skills are further developed as adults extend their questions from simple requests for labels to questions about the attributes of the items (What does the ball do? Does the ball roll because it's round?). The child is socialized into providing "reason-explanations" or commentaries. This foundation produces a particular structural feature–a socio-linguistical way of taking knowledge, managing it, and choosing a response to it. The child is taught the foundation for manipulating language to make decisions.

These literacy practices are the central structural features of standardized exams. For example, an excerpt taken from a third grade reading exam for Texas at the time of this research:

Lucy and the Chickens

"Lucy's family had lots of animals. They had cows, horses, and pigs. They also had a dog, a cat, and a bird. Lucy's favorite animals were the chickens. She enjoyed collecting eggs from the henhouse. But she wasn't allowed to gather the eggs by herself."

This is the first paragraph. The story is followed by a combination of questions, that require "what-explanations," which include answering simple who, what, when, and where questions, as well as ordering and sequencing; and "reason-explanations." For example:

1) question #1 asks: Where does Lucy live?
2) question #5 instructs: Read the chart below, it shows the order in which some of the events happen to Lucy

 – Lucy gets water for the chickens
 – Lucy opens the door to the henhouse

_____

 – Dad helps Lucy catch the chickens.

Questions #1 and 2 require a "what-explanation."

3) question #6: Why isn't Lucy allowed to gather eggs from the henhouse by herself?

However, question #3 requires a "reason-explanation."

Another example: Questions taken from an eleventh grade English Language Arts test reveal the same process on a much more advanced level. There is a story that precedes these questions, but only the questions are necessary for the examination:

Read the following dictionary entry.

fix \ ¹fiks\ v **1.** to stabilize **2.** to capture the attention of **3.** to get ready for **4.** to repair or mend

Which definition best matches the use of the word *fixed* in paragraph 8?

A. Definition 1

B. Definition 2

C. Definition 3

D. Definition 4

7. Mrs. Saroyan's statement about her son at the end of the story conveys

A. why she is dissatisfied with the way Willie manages his money

B. how she secretly wishes that Willie will become a musician

C. why she loses her temper so easily

D. how her understanding of her son has changed

In the first question the student is essentially asked "What is *this* fix?" The "what-explanation" has been extended to recognize one word can have many meanings, and the meaning is actualized by the context. The second question requires an advanced "reason-explanation" in that the student is asked to read between the lines of the whole story and determine meaning that is not explicitly stated. Both third and eleventh grade sets of questions require a sophisticated understanding and manipulation of language. The state exams, and the literacy practices that are required to successfully master them, reflect and reproduce the thoughts of the standard. The standard, however, did not originate with the School. It was produced by an ensemble of ideologies, practices, and institutions. It is in this production of the standard where these two communities diverge. The differences between the two communities lie in how they came to embody the standard and how that impacts their learning experiences.

TSU Neighborhood

In the *TSU Neighborhood*, children come home from the hospital to rooms with walls decorated with pictures based on legendary historical figures in the civil rights movement. When children are introduced to visitors, they are prompted to provide expected politeness formulas, such as "nice to meet you" and "thank you." As soon as children can talk they are reminded of these formulas in books with characters that are "polite." They are also reminded of historical characters who made personal sacrifices for the greater good of the community.

Their first books consist of the alphabet, numbers, sounds, smells and different textures for practicing motor skills (i.e. zipping zippers), and picture books of legendary historical characters. When adults read to children, they do so with the expressed purpose of preparing children to do well in school. Story-telling in the community is given only when elicited and stories are generally true (i.e., based in experience, history, or the Bible), and anything other than truth is considered a lie. Rarely do they fictionalize themselves or events; however, they do hypothesize about alternative consequences based on alternative moral choices that could be made.

The families of the *TSU Neighborhood* are extremely politically conscious about issues of race, equality, and upward mobility and they are keenly aware of the role that education plays in obtaining these ideological constructs. They are also keenly aware that these aspirations are ideological constructs.

The result in school is that many *TSU Neighborhood* children find the content of classroom lessons terribly boring and lacking the rich ideological substance they are accustomed to entertaining. Some therefore find the structure of classroom learning difficult to adjust to and are mislabeled or misdiagnosed as unable to function in the structure of a classroom. For example, in elementary school, Peter Jr. was "diagnosed" with Attention Deficit Disorder (ADD). At that time, he was attending one of the schools in Third Ward. I put the word "diagnosed" in quotations because Peter Jr.'s parents and I are skeptical of this diagnosis because it was **not identified by a certified doctor!** And that just blows my mind. The fact that a teacher who is unable to manage her classroom successfully can, with a nurse who has never examined a child, decide that the child needs to be medicated is nonsensical.

Nevertheless, the school administrator and Peter Jr.'s teacher strongly suggested that he be medicated for this "disorder." Peter Jr. was bored with the content of his classes. He completed his work quickly and then sought out other ways of entertaining himself—which were distracting to the class. Angela and Peter Sr. refused to accept the finding and declined to medicate him. Instead, they decided to move him to another school where his behavior was not described as "misbehavior," but as "normal" behavior for an eight-year-old boy. Consequently, he did exceptionally well.

ADD is a medical term, unlike *"behavior problem,"* which is a social term. With the support of hard science, a medical term makes the problem of "at-risk" a biological one. Meaning, without the support of medical science, "at-risk" as a social term is a product of how you were raised and taught to interact with society. So, a child that is "at-risk" from the perspective of a social deficiency simply hasn't been taught properly. But if it is defined as ADD, then the connotation is that there is something in the child's biology that prevents him or her from being able to perform properly. So there is a deficiency in the child's physiology. Such claims are reminiscent of the race science that circulated in the nineteenth century about the size of black people's skulls being an indicator of their intelligence. Scientific racism was used to legitimate racial biases.

George Morton, a nineteenth century scholar, measured the cranial capacity (the brain size) of skulls of blacks, native Americans, and whites in an attempt to prove that whites were superior, which he successfully proved by finding that the skulls of white people were larger.

However, approximately a century later, a Harvard biologist, Stephen Jay Gould, re-measured the same skulls used by Morton and discovered insurmountable biases in the tests. Gould describes how Morton included in his sample of skulls more black females than male skulls, he included more small-brained Inca skulls than large-brain Iroquois skulls, and he omitted small-sized Hindu skulls from his white sample. When measured without pre-conceived biases, Gould found that the average black male skull was actually larger than those of white males.

The Strivers being fully conscious of how this language game works, altered the structure of the game by removing their son from an environment that has a historical pattern of labeling African American children (especially boys) as "behavioral problems," to an environment where the energy of children is appreciated as expressions of creativity and vitality. By altering the structure of the language game, they were able to reflect the image of the standard onto themselves. Now Peter Jr. is no longer a behavioral problem, he's a normal kid. "Normalcy" is what the standard seeks to create.

The Bayou

In *The Bayou*, children come home from the hospital to an ideological standard that dates at least as far back as to the writing of the *Declaration of Independence*. Who we are as a nation was written in this document of U.S. history put forth in 1776. The introduction to the Declaration of Independence:

When in the Course of ***human*** events, it becomes necessary for *one people* to dissolve the political bands which have connected them with another, and to **assume among the powers of the earth**, the separate and equal station **to which the *Laws of Nature and of Nature's God* entitle them,** a decent respect to the opinions of mankind requires that they should declare the causes which impel them to the separation (*my emphasis in italics and bold*).

The irony here is that the signers of this document were massive slave holders; and in this document, name the inhabitants of the land before they (the signers) arrived, as "savages." However, this irony was addressed through their process of defining "human." Only "humans" were entitled to things like "liberty, justice and freedom for all," and "to assume among the powers of the earth...to which the Laws of Nature and of Nature's God entitle them." As we discussed in Chapter 1, blacks were defined as chattel (not human); and as I just pointed out, the indigenous peoples were defined as savages (not human). Therefore, only white people were the inevitable beneficiaries of the title "human." In light of this definition, color became highly contested. James Baldwin (1984) in his article *On Being White and Other Lies* argues that no one was white before coming to the U.S. They became white out of the necessity of justifying black subjugation.

A collection of terms were developed to identify people with certain percentages of "black blood," and the census was used to deliberately advance this race science by including as categories these terms in counting people. The terms *mulatto, quadroon,* and *octoroon* were some of the terms used by census takers, which had highly precise definitions, but in actual practice were used based on impressions of skin color rather than definite knowledge of ancestry. Baldwin says: "America became white. The people who as they claim settled the country became white...White men from Norway, for example where they are Norwegians, became white by slaughtering the cattle, poisoning the wells, torching the houses, massacring Native Americans, raping black women."

Each new wave of immigrants who enter the country goes through a process of being positioned into a racial group. If the skin is pale enough, they become "white." If it is not, they are essentially relegated to being "black" or "brown." Polish immigrants were once considered the "niggers" of America. Likewise the Italians, and the Irish. Over decades, however, they were "whitened."

The Manns family, with Irish roots, by virtue of the color of their skin are a picture of our "social standard." The color is "self-evident" evidence of what is described in the *Declaration of Independence* as a *natural truth*, (or a *biological truth*) that positions them in a prestigious place in the *natural order* of the standard. Remember, a standard is something considered by an authority as an "approved" model. The "authority" in this case is the *Declaration of Independence*, which effectively defines "humans" as whites–white people are the approved model for our social standard of an American. It is the basis that we used to compare all other peoples. The Manns are naturalized into the standard by the color of their skin.

In a class I taught on race, an Anglo woman from France sparked a heated debate with her classmates on the privileges of white people in America. She vehemently tried to show that she was not participating in white privilege because she has *chosen* not to. I posed this question to her: "If you and a black man are both standing on the curb hailing a cab in New York City, will the cab driver pass up the black man and stop for you? If he does, then are you not a participant whether you have chosen to be or not?" The very color of her skin has made her a participant. I am proposing the same circumstances for the Mann family.

The very color of their skin has made them *natural* heirs of the *Declaration of Independence*, because although the naming of the color of their skin as "white" is a political phenomenon, the actual color is a *natural* (biological) one. There are many co-constructors implicit in the fabric of society to this *natural heirship*, among those being the intellectual activity of standardized exams. The way of being and thinking that is legitimized by the semiotic processes of standardized exams is re-presented as inherent qualities for learning, and in their closest ideal image the inherent qualities look like the Mann family.

CHAPTER 5

The Role of Identity
in the Numbers

Identity is something that is elusive to most of us. When people ask us who we are, we generally start with our names. That name embodies a past and how we came to be in the present moment of our journey; yet we rarely think about the history that sits in the hammock of our names. But it sits nonetheless, weighing upon our every decision. Many of us spend a quarter, sometimes half or more of our lives, trying to get to know who we are. We take classes with names like: "Knowing Your Purpose," and read books with titles such as "Purpose Driven Life." As a nation, we spend billions of dollars on self-help literature and life coaches, and endless hours of time watching *Oprah's Life Class* in our efforts to understand why we may be drawn to and intuitively understand the masterpieces of Alberto Giacometti, Georgia O'Keeffe, Pablo Picasso, Frida Kahlo, Leonardo Davinci or Jean-Michel Basquiat. We may ask why we trust science to be more definitive about our world and our selves than our personal creation stories (or vice versa). We might wonder why we are prone to numbers and linear order (or just the opposite).

And then we slip into personal wonderings like why certain smells peak our interest so much that when we smell them, our heads cock to one side and we experience a euphoria that mimics orgasmic satisfaction. We might wonder why we can't stay on a job for more than three years, even when things are going well; or why it's so hard for us to leave the city we were born in for another one when the move is clearly better for the future we see in our dreams. We wonder why it's so easy to walk away from relationships once we've built familiarity. And we may ask our sisters questions like: Why do all of us like westerns when they're clearly not made for women? And there are moments when we recognize and are proud of what we're good at; and sometimes, because of who we are, we make what we're good at policy for everyone else. The modern educational system's fascination with using numbers in how we assess student performance is an example of such a course of action.

The Role of Numbers in Identity

Identity unfolds in our lives...like layers of a wrapper being peeled back from around an object. Our identity sits inside this wrapper made of something like newspaper with tiers of text imprinted upon it. These texts are social scripts that have, at different points in our life's journeys, dictated our current situation and sought to inform our futures. These texts, with creative power, shape how we see ourselves and how we re-present ourselves to others. The re-presentation of ourselves is further nurtured by those who see what we show them and this becomes who we are—whether we like it or not.

One of the layers of text is our educational system. We encounter this system for the first time very early in our lives, between the ages of three and six. We stay in this system for more than twelve years—twelve of the most formative years of life, and it is here where the layer of text begins to take form as numbers. These numbers further nurture our identity by crafting it into something that fits (whether it does or not) into a finite prescription of pre-set molds. But the numbers game didn't start here.

As a society, our fascination with numbers goes a long way back into our history as a species. We have used numbers as a scientific way of categorizing data and explaining phenomena objectively. It is a way to organize information in order to understand it and better shape it for useful purposes. It is a way to assign places to phenomena without running out of places. The infinite quality of numbers appeals to our inherent divine nature of unlimited possibilities.

The introduction of numbers into human culture was done so by way of a social evolution, not a natural one. Basic number recognition or the "sense of number" is not a sense that human infants possess at birth. But we do possess the potential to recreate the stages of evolution as it relates to concepts of civilization. But the latent ability is only developed through a process of education, whether that is done through modeling by adults or explicit teaching. "...Inventions and discoveries only get developed and adopted if they correspond to a perceived social need in a civilization. Many scientific advances are ignored if there is, as people say no 'call' for them." (Ifrah, 1987) . In the cultures of most of the peoples around the world who were conquered by other civilizations whose values and traditions have endured through hundreds of years of evolution, there was no need for numbers to evolve to the abstract. However, because the culture that conquered was considered superior by the very fact that they successfully conquered another group, their traditions were also regarded as superior. Therefore, groups like the Aborigines, Pygmies, Polynesians and Indigenous peoples to the Americas were labeled as "primitive" because they did not engage in the abstraction of numbers.

The history of numbers is a distinct human and cultural evolutionary event. Natural human ability to perceive numbers does not exceed the number four. Take a look at the illustration below, and with one glance try to estimate the number of objects in each set. But you must do it with ONE visual glance.

Everyone can with one glance estimate those sets that include one, two, three and most people can see the set of four, but above that the quantities become vague, and our eyes alone cannot tell us how many things there are. We need to group them in twos, threes, or fours in order to estimate how many there are. We cannot just see the answers; we must "count" them to know how many there are. Therefore, the ability to "count" is not an innate ability. It is a "learned" ability.

The Problem with Numbers in the School

As I said earlier, identity is one of those things that is rooted in a lot of subconscious history. I've always loved math, but I don't really get it. I find numbers incredibly efficient, but also unbelievably artful. When I'm faced with a numbers problem I find myself gazing at it like gazing at a masterful piece of art; and I wonder: *Where did that come from?* I've never understood that dichotomy of loving math and not understanding it until I read *A Universal History of Numbers*. As I trekked back into history to try to more fully understand my fascination with numbers, I learned that math was not always done with numbers. As a matter of fact, numbers and mathematics are not necessarily the same thing. Before numbers, math was done with scenario stories. And peoples of African descent were masters of this process. That skill has been passed on, embodied in the flesh of generations along with the importance of relationship. This model of scenario/story math is directly linked to the process of building, sustaining, and engaging a relationship model. Understanding this model is critical in understanding how to engage students of color in learning. What I discovered about my own learning process is that what I love about math is actually the numbers.

I love numbers. I love the idea of them. I love the abstract nature of numbers. I love what you can do with their abstract nature. I love how you can use them to pinpoint critical parts on the body that can be manipulated for healing purposes, and how you can use them to tell mystical, mythical, spiritual, and universal stories. The concept of numbers is essentially a language. It is a language that can be used to talk about abstract notions. "For Plato numbers constituted 'the highest degree of knowledge' and made up the essence of inner and outer harmony" (Ifrah, 1987). Numbers in and of themselves are abstract disembodied figures that are used to represent exact thought. And this is why I love them so much. I use numbers to talk about those things that are not concrete–those things that are not tangible. Numbers are a language. Thus, my love for them–I have a deep attraction to languages.

Now, having understood that, I can begin to think about math as a language and that, in and of itself, will make math easier for me to understand. What if we instituted this type of teaching for the children of my primary case study? In failing schools across the country, what if we began to discover the things that the students have always been fascinated by and use that fascination to help them do "required learning"? Wow. It would be a spectacular display of holistic teaching and learning. It is very similar to what my five colleagues and I did in the middle school that we started in New York City (which I discussed in the Preface).

The problem we are facing in public education today is that we are trying to change the situation of high-poverty, marginalized kids of urban public schools of color by trying to change their identities *from* whatever it is *to* the "approved" model for our social standard of what it means to be an American. We create curricula that appreciate the customs, practices, skills and traditions of European histories and relegate the histories of black and Latino students to *extra*-curricular or non-academic programs; or we have removed them from the school entirely. These policies unfortunately *create* identities instead of defining our conditions.

As a consequence, we have peoples who have been defined as "Poor" instead of defining the *living condition* as one of *poverty*. The difference is it is very hard to change the identity of a person, and so we have many failed policies designed to address the issues of the poor. However, it is a lot easier to change the condition of poverty by equalizing access to resources, providing a distribution system that is just by leveling the playing field of capitalism for everyone to have an equal chance to start at the same starting line. But when we focus on trying to change the identity of the person, we are really trying to change the physiology of the substance or the essence of the spirit. That can only be done by the

131

individual from the inside of his own being. But we can help him by changing the structures that oppress him.

Instead of changing the structures that oppress public school students, we establish structures that seek to suppress those things that have had pivotal roles for centuries in shaping who they are.

For example, music for hundreds of years has been a socio-linguistical way of communicating vital information among African American communities. During the African slave period in America, songs were used to communicate strategic escape plans through a sophisticated coding system that held information about when, where, and how to escape slavery. Songs have also been used to exchange secret messages among slaves that served as warnings of potentially dangerous encounters, as well as possibilities of hope. These songs were specifically designed to counter unequal structural platforms that denied black peoples the most basic human rights (like the rights to learn and to freedom). As I pointed out in Chapter 3, most of the children of *The Bottoms* (who still operate in many of these traditions) have memorized the lyrics of entire songs by the time they turn two years old. It is a tradition that has become not only embedded in the community, but also in the personality (and the *learning personality*) of the members of the community.

If we devalue this form of communication (manipulating language through music, art, and movement) by relegating it to an extracurricular process at best and completely removing it from the school at worst, in favor of solely practicing a different linguistical syntactical process (such as manipulating language on worksheets), we are not simply teaching, but we are actually struggling to reshape the very flesh, or the substance of the individual that has taken hundreds of years to shape. This is why it has been so difficult to institute educational reforms that produce transformative outcomes for the kids that the reforms have sought to help. Every seven to ten years, we come out with a new standardized test that is designed to address inherent biases of the previous one. But African American students in mass have never done well on any of these tests. It is because we are focusing on trying to change their identities, rather than trying to change their condition.

One of the prominent leaders of the charter school movement in New Orleans, LA has done some great work in reforming the public school system in that city after Hurricane Katrina. Reports show the movement has been successful in raising achievement scores of students by twenty-four percent, city-wide. The city has gone from neighborhood zoned schools to an open school choice plan. Students (families) can submit an application to go to any school in the city. I recently had the chance to hear him present his data. It is very encouraging data, with the lines on the charts steadily going upwards. He was very humble in admitting he thought that though they have done some good work (increasing student performance scores), there was still much more to do. They are working towards a full choice school district, in which every parent has the choice to choose which school their children attend. He said that in a system such as this, every "bad" school should "naturally" close, because parents are not choosing them.

But he admitted that that was not the case. Parents are still pretty overwhelmingly choosing schools that are considered by reformers, policy makers, the media, and me as "bad." These are schools that produce valedictorians who cannot pass a national standardized exam or who cannot pass a remedial college reading, writing, or math class. He admitted that they had not taken into account the historical importance of the neighborhood school to the community or the importance of school bands in a city literally built by music. To his credit, that was an amazing level of sensitivity for someone who did not come from the experience of the community he had been hired to reform. He is like most of the national faces of education reform today–they come from different conditional backgrounds and typically launch well intentioned education reforms that unintentionally widens the achievement possibilities between students of color and Anglo students.

You see, this charter school leader (not unlike his colleagues) says that he looks at whatever wealthy people do for their children's educational situation and works to create those same opportunities for under-served communities. This is the crux of the problem. When we seek to import other peoples' value systems onto people with a different value system, it will never work. The value systems of wealthy Anglo people are driven by numbers. The value systems of most African Americans are driven by relationships. Extended communal relationships that are built in school bands, neighborhood schools, and schools that embody an energy that makes the families feel like they belong, generally supersede the numbers game for underserved African American families.

Numbers...Evolution...Math

For Pythagoras, numbers help to articulate the abstract elements of the universe. For prehistoric peoples, the use of numbers was for very specific concrete needs and concerns, like determining how much the neighboring village owed you for reparations of warriors lost in a skirmish, or when the next sacred celebration would take place. They did not "count" per say, but they used a one-to-one mapping process. For example, they used a "body-counting" system, in which they:

"...touched each other's right-hand fingers, starting with the little finger, then the right wrist, elbows, shoulder, ear, and eye. Then they touched each other's nose, mouth then the left eye, ear, shoulder elbows, and wrist, and on to the little finger of the left hand, getting to 22 so far. If the number needed is higher, they go on to the breasts, hips, and genitals, then the knees, ankles and toes on the right then the left side. This extension allows 19 further integers, or a total of 41" pg 15. "Using joints and knuckles increases the possible range, and it allowed the Ancient Egyptians, the Romans, the Arabs and the Persians (not forgetting Western Christians in the Middle Ages) to represent concretely all the numbers from 1 to 9,999. An even more ingenious variety of finger-reckoning allowed the Chinese to count to 100,000 on one hand and to one million using both hands!" (Ifrah, 1987)

The body-counting points are however not thought of by their users as "numbers," but rather as the points that represent a notion arrived at after a synchronized sequence of body-gestures. This means that the mere designation of any one of the points is not sufficient to describe a given number unless the term uttered is accompanied by the corresponding sequence of gestures. So in discussion concerning a particular number, no real "number-term" is uttered. Instead a given number of body-counting points are itemized, alongside the simultaneous sequence of gestures. It is therefore important to *see* the speaker in order to know what has been communicated. The process of communicating these "numbers" cannot be divorced from the "numbers" themselves, nor can the objects that are used to associate the one-for-one comparison of numbers be disconnected from the "number." The people did not abstract the "points" in the numbering sequence; the sequence remained embedded in the specific nature of the "points" themselves.

Understanding how prehistoric peoples used numbers explains a lot about how both I and my students were relating to numbers. Western civilizations developed the need to evolve from using concrete objects in a one-to-one comparison for tallying (with their hands, their bodies, tally sticks, knotted strings, and pebbles) to using "numeration" or letters, words, and figures to represent the abstract concept of a number. But many eastern, African, and indigenous American cultures remained connected to concrete one-to-one mapping processes even today. These peoples and their descendants find it next to impossible to detach numbers from the objects or processes represented by the numbers. So, to ask children, whose history is embedded with this understanding, to engage with abstract disconnected number symbols is asking a whole lot more than we realize.

As an educator who works with kids who descended from non-Western cultures, and as a descendent of one of those non-Western cultures myself, I have found both my own and my students' appreciation of numbers more instinctively aligned to the non-Western historical understanding of the language of numbers. And yet, as a researcher I have also found the Western use of numbers very efficient. However, I find the Western use to be more effective when exercised from the non-Western historical perspective that is akin to what has become embedded, literally, in my flesh (i.e. the one-to-one mapping of quantities of things through the body-counting method).

Numeration made counting easier; but the invention of zero exponentially advanced the language of numbers to the concept of math. "You could say that the history of numbering systems fills the space between One and Zero–the two concepts which have become the symbols of modern technological society." (Ifrah, 1987)

This very abstract concept that we call Zero is where mathematics comes from. It is with the introduction of mathematics, that numbers began to be so singularly connected to math.

Over many moments of evolutionary advance we have come to a place today in our educational system where we primarily only talk about numbers in math class, and we only talk about education reform in numbers.

The numbers have been completely detached from our concrete use of them in our everyday and relegated only to a decontextualized disconnected isolated environment, so much so that children are failing miserably at grasping the concept; and more egregiously, educational reform measures are using numbers to "identify" kids as "at risk" and "unacceptable." Also equally egregious, some education reform entities are using these disconnected disembodied numbers to tell very heavily manipulated success stories.

The Role of Identity in Numbers

KIPP (the Knowledge is Power Program) is a national charter school entity with amazing number stories of urban kids of color from communities that typically score very, very low on state tests, performing highly on state performance exams. However, I came across in article in The Washington Post about a policy that KIPP practices, which makes these number stories suspicious (http://www.washingtonpost.com/wp-dyn/content /article/2007/04/24/AR2007042400558.html?referrer =emailarticle). Potential leaders for KIPP schools go through the KIPP training program, and after successfully completing the program they open a KIPP school. The name of the school is the KIPP XX School. The XX is up to the leader. It may be called the "KIPP Sharon School". As a KIPP school, it is understood to have certain expectations in place. For example, logistically all KIPP schools have a longer than traditional school day and school year that provides more time for students to catch up on the things they are missing when they enter a KIPP program. All KIPP schools receive additional funding from the KIPP foundation to support the extra help students need to catch up. And to that end, all KIPP students must meet certain performance expectations. If the students do not meet these expectations, the central office provides support to the leader to help her get the students' test scores up. However, if after working with a school leader for two or more years and the students' test scores are still below KIPP's expectations, KIPP will take their name from the school. It is no longer a KIPP school.

A couple of things happen: For one, all that goes along with being "named" a KIPP school goes with the name. If you are a parent and you have gone through the rigorous application process to enroll your child into a program with the KIPP name and while your child is in the school, that name is stripped away that can be a disorienting experience. Secondly, when KIPP takes the name from a school the performance scores of those students are not counted when KIPP evaluates their success. If you only count the students who do well in your program, of course your program will perform well.

The discovery of "counting is what allowed people to take the measure of their world" (Ifrah, 1987). Eventually people began to define their identity by their possessions that they could count. In the example of KIPP, the only thing that will cause KIPP to take their name from a school that they have opened is that the students are not meeting performance scores expectations. KIPP has defined itself by their high performing test scores. If students are not producing high test scores, it appears they cannot be called KIPP students.

The role of numbers in the identity of those who make policy today in education is as "natural" for them as it is "unnatural" for the students who are being shaped by these numbers into categories of "unacceptable" and "at-risk." However, because the policy makers have a natural kinship to numbers, it is widely accepted as the most advanced, the most efficient way and the "*norm*" of doing education today. Education today is discussed in the language of numbers. The exact nature of numbers allows education to shape an exact identity of its constituents. It opens up the possibility of clearly distinguishing one entity from another, one group from another, but most importantly of determining the value of one group, idea, or concept over another. This practice of using numbers goes so far back into the history of Western cultures, and it is so integrated into our way of thinking that it is seen as an innate characteristic of being human, like walking upright on two feet.

Ifrah (1987) says: "Decisive progress towards the art of abstract calculation that we now use could only be made once it was clearly understood that the integers could be classified into a hierarchized system of numerical units whose terms were related as kinds within types, types within species, and so on..." In 1057, Aristotle referred to this principal as "recurrence." The German philosopher Schopenhauer put it this way: "Any natural integer presupposes its preceding numbers as the cause of its existence."

This is a very profound understanding of one's very existence. This understanding has molded the identity of those who embrace it. It has so affected the identity that the identity believes it cannot exist without it. This is the identity that has crafted our current educational system. Without the numbers we essentially do not exist.

These are the attitudes that are shaping policy for public education students—most of whom come from a different value system of numbers. This Western value system is imposing upon public education students not only a requirement to think differently (which in and of itself is a monumental task) but to BE different, which is an identity shaping project. It is certainly a project that has happened repeatedly throughout history. Whether it has been successful depends on how you define success. However, it is clearly failing our public school system, as we have a dropout rate of twenty to fifty percent across our nation.

A Place to Which Every Work Is Assigned...

Everything we do or don't do is encapsulated in our identities. Our identity is the substance that holds these works, and like a glass that holds a beautiful rose colored tea, our identity shapes the work we do.

In our society we essentially have square blocks that people are put into, either by themselves or by others. In fact, the process is a co-constructing process that involves the history, the present condition, and the hope of future expectations of the individual, her collective identity as a member of a cultural group based on gender, family, race, etc. These blocks are constantly moving and shifting because we are inherently dynamic. Life is constantly shifting. However, these blocks shift, still intact, and they move across generations of time. For people who have found themselves in blocks that determine the value of all blocks, they are generally content with their space. But for those who find themselves in a block that is being determined by others, they look for ways to break out. The people who are defining what School looks like today are people who engage with numbers in a very different way than their constituents. The results are what we see in our failing public schools today.

In one such school in Houston, TX, the graduation rate is at about forty percent. The state has placed heavy sanctions on the district to reverse that trend. I'm an education anthropologist, and I work in the trenches of urban education, working to turn around the worst performing schools in a district. So I was hired to implement new systemic processes for the campus. There were also lots of other consultants, state conservators, and auditors on that campus. One consultant (a white woman whose background in education is centered in suburban education) was hired to prepare teachers to prepare students for the new state standardized test that was coming the following year. She made a comment that indicated she would not be able to help turn this situation around. She made the comment because the school was a buzz about homecoming (the teachers were as excited as the students), and for the most part there was little to no traditional academic learning happening the entire week before the event. Her remark was: "The teachers are so far behind, they don't even know how to develop a lesson plan. The kids are performing lower than I can even imagine, but instead of focusing on the homework that they've been given, they're all focused on homecoming!"

Another consultant (a black man from New York University, and whose educational background is centered in urban education) criticized our colleague as being completely out of touch with the reality of the lives of these students. He said she had an elitist attitude that made it impossible for her to actually see the people she's supposed to help as "actual people." According to him, she saw them as "stereotypes," playing "roles" that she had "heard about." Therefore she would never be able to truly help them, because they are not simply characters that she's seen in badly written movies or in handcuffs on the ten o'clock news, but they are individuals with a history that she had no knowledge of. I thought about both perspectives. The suburban consultant was certainly telling the truth. The teachers are unbelievably behind. In fact, so behind in their own learning processes that I question how they met the qualifications to be teachers. I mean, I would not be surprised if they had gotten someone else to take the certification test for them. The students were equally significantly behind by two or more years. And yet, there was something culturally intrinsically important about the urban consultant's point of view.

The tradition of celebrating homecoming for schools is a time for alumni to return to the school in a tradition of pride that expresses value and significance. There are cultural and sports events and an election of the homecoming queen and king. It's a commonly celebrated custom in North American schools. However, like the history of music for black Americans, the homecoming celebration has a deeper meaning for these peoples who descended from enslaved peoples. The concept of "home" has a deeply rooted pathology associated with not really having one.

Black Americans have never been truly integrated into the ideology of what it means to be "American." The best that has happened is to be black or African American. But not just American. Furthermore, African Americans as a group have not been accepted by Africans as *truly* African, because for 400 years they have been away from the land, and the customs and the values of what it means to be African. Moreover, during the days of enslaved black peoples in this country, black families were not allowed to participate in the traditional definition of "family" because offspring and spouses were subject to being sold at the slave owner's discretion. Therefore, biological families were often separated, and socially constructed families replaced those natural ties. So, "home" has been an internal struggle that has been addressed with new definitions of connections to space, place, time and experience.

"For African Americans, home is a continuum of experiences—a celebration of memories, stream of interactions, and a cacophony of feelings. It is a line of broken and unbroken relationships, and a circle of life filled with trials, tribulations and hallelujah moments. It is even more; home for us is a symphony of beliefs—a visible and invisible chain of human history that is imprinted on the DNA of each black congregant. And, yes, home is a human library of black hopes, dreams, disappointments, failures, successes, and achievements—personal and public. It is an ancestral map of lost tribes, muted tongues, forgotten civilizations, discarded gods, and transformed lives. It is built, brick-by-brick, by each congregant, family and community. Home, for all African Americans, is both a fixed and portable concept. However, every now and then, we have to go back to the old landmark, to that fixed place and commune together." (Ralph Wheeler, 2008).

Like music, homecoming is one of those social scripters that has both strategically grounded this group in a place from which they engage with and make sense of reality, and simultaneously shaped their identity. In turn, homecoming is a social script that has been shaped by the people's need to create normalcy and legacy. So, while I agree with my colleague that academic performance is in a critical state at this school and critically important in general, I also urge us to consider that unless we understand the historically situated socio-cultural formations that have prescribed the values that we disdain, we will not be able to transform the dismal academic predicament. We must appreciate the value of one's history in order to excavate those healing components of it and make use of them to move a people out of a place that we all agree is unacceptable.

CHAPTER 6

The Conclusion

Learned Powerlessness in The Bottoms

At the start of my research seven years ago, I met "Jasmine" while walking through the neighborhood that I had moved into to help build educational opportunities for the children of the community. One cold Sunday morning in January 2005, Jasmine, the twenty-three-year-old mother of three children under the age of three, and the housemate of "Pickles", the twenty-year-old mother of two children under the age of four, stood on the front lawn of the house they were renting, screaming at these children: "What the fuck are you crying bout? Imo beat cho ass. You gitten on my damn nerves with all that fuckin crying." The temperature was in the low forties and the babies were wearing only diapers, no shoes, no tops, no pants, no jackets. Their noses were running as they stood on the lawn, shaking like leaves on a tree when the wind was blowing, while their mother and aunt screamed profanities at them.

This scene is eerily reminiscent of another scene pictured in our history: a scene of African peoples stripped naked and standing on an auction block. These peoples were slaves, which in this country denotes that they were property, without rights, capabilities, or dignity. They were without humanness, treated like animals; *taught* to react with *instinctual* behavior. By that, I mean rather than teaching the peoples the language and customs of the land through an analytical process such as through schooling, the slave owners and overseers simply beat them when they did something wrong. Thus, the peoples learned to "react" to "mistakes." Customs were learned and managed through brutal physical punishment–through violence and the use of violent language.

I was walking with the pastor of the church that you met at the beginning of this book (she is the one who holds a reading program every summer for the children surrounding her church and is also the mother of the black family of my comparative case study, Rev. Dr. "Angela Strivers"). After church was over, she went back to check on the five small children–the children standing on the front lawn in the forty degree weather in nothing but diapers. We discovered that there were actually from nine to eleven children and from two to four "adults" living in the small five-room shotgun house on any given day. I enclosed the word "adults" in quotations because they were not led into the maturity that comes with being an adult. They just got bigger and older, and eventually moved into their own house, bringing up their children in the same way they were brought up. The stability of the home is constantly threatened, as people come and go. At the time of this research, living in the house, were Jasmine and her five children, her friend (aka her "cousin") Pickles with her two children, and Jasmine's brother and his girlfriend and their two children.

That cold Sunday morning in January when we met Jasmine, she was on her way somewhere, and the children followed her outside to try and go with her. She had told them to go back inside and they started crying. Two of her children had been irritable for quite some time, and Jasmine was leaving the house to get away from the regular madness of the household. The children wanted to go with her. She exploded. The children "made" her lose her temper.

On another occasion, Jasmine's brother and his girlfriend had a fight. He was extremely violent with his girlfriend. During the fight they were throwing things at one another and one of the things landed in the yard of their next door neighbor. It was a butcher's knife. The neighbor, who is a member of Pastor Angela's church, told the landlord, who called Jasmine. Jasmine was furious. Pastor Angela went over to talk to Jasmine to run interference between Jasmine and the member of her church.

Jasmine: That old lady needs to mind her own business and um gonna go tell her that.

Pastor: That may be true if you can keep your business over here...if we couldn't hear what was going on over here. But when a butcher's knife lands in her yard there's a problem.

Jasmine: My brother and his girlfriend are grown, and I can't tell them what to do.

Pastor: But this is your house and your children are here; and you mean to tell me that if people are cussing and fighting in front of them, you can't stop them from doing it in your house?

Jasmine looked as though she had been introduced to a new thought. Jasmine, like the Freeman family and those they represent, have emotional love for their children, but they have been shaped by a violence-affirming environment of oppression. Violent language is a part of their everyday language, it is not intentional abuse. The behavior of "people coming in and out of the house" is part of their everyday living. It is not understood as unstable. And violence is the way they, like their former oppressors (the slave masters), manage behavior.

Freire points out in his work, *Pedagogy of the Oppressed*, that "the great humanistic and historical task of the oppressed is to liberate themselves and their oppressors as well" (Freire, 1970). Freire was extremely concerned with *praxis*, or action that is informed and linked to certain values, of which an important element is *conscientization*, or developing a consciousness that is understood to have the power to transform reality. In other words, in order for true liberation to happen, the oppressed must not become like the oppressors. They must develop a consciousness that can transform the reality of the present despite the reality of history. The families in *The Bottoms* have not developed that kind of consciousness. Their struggle has been concentrated on getting "things."

The Civil Rights Movement of the 1950s and 1960s transformed a concrete situation of oppression (racism) by establishing a process of liberation through the changing of segregationists' laws. Abolishing the "separate but equal" laws in the use of public facilities from bathrooms and water fountains to buses and trains, and the access to public institutions from libraries to schools set the stage for change in the thought processes of individuals. But for many African Americans, the struggle was reduced to things; for example, their struggle was reduced to simply having *access* to schools, instead of being creative participants in the structure of School. It is essential for the oppressed to realize that when they accept the struggle for becoming more fully human they also accept total responsibility for the struggle. They must realize that they are fighting not merely for freedom to go to school, but for

...freedom to create and to construct, to wonder and to venture. Such freedom requires that the individual be active and responsible, not a slave or a well-fed cog in the machine.... It is not enough that men are not slaves; if social conditions further the existence of automatons, the result will not be love of life, but love of death. (Freire 1970)

The black families of the *TSU Neighborhood* understand this concept; the black families of *The Bottoms* do not. Families in *The Bottoms* have abdicated too much responsibility through a process of self-depreciation. They have been told by numerous ideologies and institutions (slavery, media images, political policies, self-images) that they are incapable, dumb, and irresponsible, that they will never amount to anything; and they have believed it. Convinced of their own unfitness, they have left the job of education completely up to the School, so much so that they are annoyed if anyone tries to involve them in the matters of the School in any way other than complaining and blaming.

The behavior of these families is a "prescribed" behavior that they have internalized and adopted as a principle. It is a behavior that we have encountered as a consequence of institutionalized racism. Racism as an institution establishes the ideology of race as a biological occurrence (you are born a "black" or "white" person), then biologically categorizes people into a system of hierarchy designed to undermine the self-image of marginalized peoples. These self-images of incapable, powerlessness, intellectually deficient, and physically unattractive are validated through established customs in our society.

Racism was embedded in our society through avenues as comprehensive and diverse as the scientific community, the federal census, marriage laws, employment applications, birth certificates, school curricula, media images of crime, police racial profiling, and on and on. The tenets are so varied and spread out that it is impossible to point to one agent as a central figure. It is simply recognized by communities (all over the U.S.) like *The Bottoms* as a system that they cannot break out of. Although concrete changes have been made in the laws that supported racism, the spirit of the institution continues in the consciousness of these families. They have reduced themselves, like their struggles, to *objects* to be had and to be acted *upon*, rather than as persons who act upon objects. Their behavior is one of *learned powerlessness*.

Learned Powerlessness

We have looked in the previous chapters in some detail through case study at the experiences and cultural processes of these families on the one hand, exercising real power in their choice to make the School solely responsible for their children's learning. On the other hand, we have seen their genuinely held convictions lead to a place of entrapment instead of liberation, producing a cultural pattern of failure for themselves and their children. Consequently, they see themselves as powerless. The external limitations prevent and distort their worldview of themselves. Being without a high school education, without money, without access to money, without proper housing, without public transportation in their community, without decent grocery stores, without the help of the second parent, they see themselves without the "things" that would make them "somebody." "I wanna be somebody," Kenny Freeman once said as he was telling me his dream for his life, which included having a certain kind of car, house, job–"things."

In their worldview they lack the capability to affect the realities of their world. They have no say over whether they will get the job they want, how their loved ones act toward them; no ability to change their own addictive behaviors, to change how past negative events affect them today, to ensure that their dreams come true, or to change things that they have repeatedly attempted to change with no success. In their worldview, the capability to make these changes is entwined with having "things." And since they do not have "things," they do not have the power to make changes.

This is very obviously a learned sense of powerlessness because it is so wrapped up in "objects." It has deep roots in the history of this country with regard to how we measure success. Historically the black community, before integration, no matter how much education one had or what kind of job one had, all lived in the same neighborhood, basically with the same kind of house. The way that African Americans showed difference in their situations was in the kind of car they had, the clothes they could afford, the furniture in the house–the "things" they had. In a world where you are conditioned to gauge your own progress by competing with your neighbors or colleagues, or you feel better about your own misery by contending that there are others worst off than you, "things" take on a significance that is equated with inherent qualities of goodness and of humanness.

The meaning that is embedded in such a way of thinking will have profound effects on behavior. If these families equate "things" with inherent qualities of being human, then their assumptions about what it is to be human will include a ravenous quest for "things" at all cost. The process of going through school to acquire these "things" is often too slow for these families. Most don't expect to live pass thirty years of age. Many do not–they are murdered. Many others are imprisoned. They cannot see why staying in school would improve their situation. Consequently, they find themselves involved in illegal means of making money in order to get "things." And in their worldview, those "things" include each other.

Kenny Freeman said:

I just didn't know my mother that well until I turn around fourteen years old. I also didn't have a father or didn't even know my father, and right now today, I still don't know my father. I...didn't get the things I wanted like shoes and things what other kids had...But...I think the things I really need is a mother and father in my life.

Things are objects to be had; they are not responsible "agents" (or people) with transformative power. This is the "worldview" of the families of *The Bottoms*: They have learned to see themselves in the world as things: as without the possibility for collective action to change norms, as only constrained and not also enabled in the pursuit of their goals, as merely the effects of structures, not agents with "power" to affect outcomes. This is clearly not the case, because their behavior (their agency) with the School has crippled the schools in *The Bottoms*. No amount of reform has helped these schools, because parents are not sharing in the responsibility for their children's school learning.

Agency is not only in operation when we are aware of it. Agency is at work whenever one or more persons has the ability to affect the outcome of a situation, regardless of whether or not they intend to–regardless of whether they are aware that these outcomes are occurring. And although the parents of *The Bottoms* are not aware of their agency, it is affecting the School. They are demonstrating agency in the way they are interpreting the *educational contract.* As we have discussed, they have decided that education is something for the School to handle, so they have relinquished responsibility and placed the accountability for ensuring their children are educated solely on the School. Again, however, it is important to point out that this behavior is not just a simple "giving up," but it was learned through a long historical process that began with slavery and the use of violence to manage behavior, and continued through history with institutional racism that rendered them irrelevant in the School.

There is hope, however. Because it is a *learned behavior,* it can be *unlearned.* Nevertheless, before the unlearning can take place a few things must be in position. First of all, these families must understand "power" differently. Power is a spiritual quality that we all embody. I, like Foucault, believe that power should be understood as a force that is exercised from infinite points in an unequal interplay of constantly changing relations. Therefore, if we find ourselves in a relationship in which another is controlling our thoughts and actions or is determining our destiny, it is because we have "allowed" ourselves this position in the relationship—we have consented to or tolerated our position. I, like Paulo Freire, believe: "Only power that springs from the weakness of the oppressed is sufficiently strong enough to liberate both the oppressed and the oppressor." Therefore power has to be a spiritual quality that can be focused to do whatever one wants it to do. With this new understanding of power, these families would be able to see how "powerfully" they are affecting the outcomes of their children's school life, by not being involved. They would be able to see that they not only have the capacity to make change in their home-life, but that they are affecting the actions that occur, by "allowing" such actions. They would be able to understand that they can change institutions that have been for decades (in some cases centuries) rendering them into hopeless neighborhoods, schools, and futures.

Second, these families must understand that the structure of their thought has been conditioned by a concrete historical reality, and their perception of themselves as oppressed is weakened by their submersion in the reality of the oppression. By that, I mean, while they must see themselves as oppressed (because if they do not they will become comfortable with their condition), they must not see themselves as victims. To see themselves as victims produces a mentality of entitlement to *gifts*. Transformation cannot be given; it must be acquired, constantly and responsibly.

Third, the families must critically recognize the causes of their oppression, so that through transforming action they can create a new situation that makes it possible to pursue a fuller humanity. By that, I mean the goal is to see themselves as "human" (not "things"). But their only example of what "human" looks like is their oppressors. Frantz Fanon, Martinican psychiatrist and philosopher of colonialism, made a profound prediction in the 1960s. It was a time when colonialism was falling apart in African nations. He predicted that if the African leaders who were rising up to recapture their homelands from colonial nations, did not also recapture or recreate a distinctly African identity, then they would, in fact, become like the colonizers. Furthermore, because the African leaders grew up in the colonial system, which was a system that created in black peoples a *fragmentation of the self* as you are compelled to become assimilated into a politics of whiteness that obliges you to disconnect from everything that you are as a black person, Fanon predicted that these African leaders would become worse than the colonizers in brutality, greed, and dysfunctionality of rule.

He predicted this scenario because the revolutionary leaders knew no other way of being, except the brutal dictatorial rule of leaders who raped the land of all natural and human resources. Therefore, these upcoming African leaders would imitate the only form of leadership they had come to know, and they would be better at it, because it is the only thing they have ever known. Fanon's prediction was spot on. Likewise, families in *the bottoms* of cities across the country have fallen prey to similar dysfunction–meaning they have learned from their experiences as victims of violence to manage their own and their children's lives with violence. African Americans have been fighting to be more fully human since the proclamation, by our nation, that they would be recognized as "three fifths of a person." But for the families in *The Bottoms*, they have not discovered what it is to be human outside of their own experiences with violence.

They are suffering from a duality in which "to be" is "to be like," and "to be like" is "to be like the one who provided this model" of violent dehumanization (the oppressor).

For example, the idea of "beating" one's children dates back to the days of slaves getting "beatings" for "misbehavior"; and the idea of others "making" you lose your temper also dates back to the same days when justifying black subjugation was done by denying personal responsibility for one's participation in the institution of racism. Personal responsibility was denied by attributing slavery to "cultural norms" for a particular time.

Pedagogy of the Masses: a grassroots pedagogy

These three factors are part of the tragic dilemma of the oppressed, which their education must take into account. Freire terms such an education: Pedagogy of the oppressed. It is a pedagogy that must be built *with*–not *for*–the oppressed (whether peoples or individuals). Such pedagogy would make oppression and its causes objects of reflection for the oppressed, and from that reflection they can engage in the struggle for their liberation. Freire says: "The pedagogy of the oppressed...is the pedagogy of people engaged in the fight for their own liberation..." And those who recognize, or begin to recognize, themselves as oppressed must be among the developers of this pedagogy.

No pedagogy which is truly liberating can remain distant from the oppressed by treating them as unfortunates and by presenting for their emulation models from among the oppressors. The oppressed must be their own example in the struggle for their redemption," (Freire, 1970).

So how do we achieve this kind of participation? The process of transformation cannot be a monologue delivered by the School, but it must be a dialogue first amongst the families themselves, then between them and the School. The families must critically confront reality. By that, I mean they must simultaneously objectify and subjectively act upon that reality. In other words, the historical reality of racist oppression must be acted upon objectively.

It should be approached as a system that can be changed. The system, or the component of the institution of racism in this country that we are concerned with here is the School System. The School is a very formidable opponent to these families, and so we must first make a distinction between the *education system*—which can only be changed by political will, and *educational projects,* which should be carried out *with* the oppressed in the process of organizing them—it is a pedagogy of the masses, using a grassroots approach.

For example, on the eve of the publication of this book, I had a conversation with a very good friend who was in an urgent situation to find a school for her son.

My friend grew up in Third Ward, in the *TSU Neighborhood,* and she said with a sigh: "Why is it that all of these years later, we are still having the same problem of finding a good middle school in our neighborhood? When I was growing up, there wasn't a good middle school option. And today, I am in this predicament of trying to find a school for my son." I said to her: Ironically that's what I'm writing about now. She said: "If you find the answer, please let me know." Again ironically, as I talked to her about the situation, it became clear to me that *she* is the answer.

Parents like my friend, parents with a sense of conscientization, put their children in schools outside of their neighborhood; therefore, the neighborhood schools have lost a critical base for proper functionality. If all of the parents who drove their children to schools in predominantly white neighborhoods would come together as a collective, and together decide that they will put their children in the neighborhood school as a collective, that act would come with certain expectations for the school that these parents would without question hold the school to, and the school would in turn change.

Parents' involvement, on any scale, would change their schools more than any top down reform effort could ever hope to do. However, education reform typically does not come from the sensibility of those who need the reform. For example, In the 1960s a new wave of "progressive" education was born. It is known as the "whole language" reading model. Educators such as Jonathan Kozol complained about the irrelevance of curriculum, meaningless routines, dehumanizing discipline, lock-step schedules, and schools' roles in perpetuating inequality. Vestiges of the earlier progressive movements, such as the Quakers who used project-based learning, narrative report cards, small-group instruction, student involvement in choosing activities, and flexible use of space were brought into public school classrooms.

However, unlike the Quakers, this new progressive movement asserted that learning to read should be like learning to talk—a "natural" process. The proponents of this movement had great intentions of enhancing the lives of many urban public school students of color. The

California school system instituted this methodology in almost all of their schools. The state government offered very enticing money incentives for all school districts that would agree to take it on. Only one district refused to take it. And it is the only district that did not go under. All of the districts that took on the new program had horrendous results.

The problem with the methodology is that it is designed for a certain kind of student, one who has been read to by adults at home from the womb–it is designed for the students of my comparative case studies, not for students who come from places like *The Bottoms*. The home of the ideal student for this program is book centered, and reading for the sake of reading is a part of their way of life. For someone who grew up in a home like this, reading would seem like a "natural" process–like talking. Advocates of the program attempted to apply this theory of "natural" process to learning to read. The idea was that the skills for reading would come "naturally" as children just read, the way that we learn to talk.

The problem is that talking is not a "natural" process. We either learn to talk by listening to others, or we are explicitly taught to talk by adults who take babbling sounds of babies and turn them into words and extend them into fully formed sentences.

Now having misunderstood the very foundation of their theory, proponents of "whole language" doomed many black children to social promotion (passing students to the next grade because they are too old to be retained any longer) and eventually graduating without knowing how to read or write. There was no focus on learning the skills that were supposed to be "natural." Consequently, if students did not come to school with these skills, they could not succeed in this method of learning because they had to first be taught the skills. But because the skills were such a "natural" way of being for the designers of this curriculum, the students who did not have the skills were thought to be "learning disabled" or "special education" cases.

The state of California was the hardest hit with this debacle, but the program was instituted all across the country, from California to New York, covering all the large urban cities in between. It was disastrous. As a result, in the late 1970s and early 1980s, there was an outcry from reformers, politicians, and parents and the "back-to-basics" movement was born. This movement calls for refocusing on the reading skills that are needed to be a proficient reader, including phonics, vocabulary building and spelling, and reading comprehension skills. The movement came with many state minimum competency standardized tests to ensure high school graduates' mastery of basic reading, writing, and math skills. These tests have been constantly remade as "biases" are discovered and argued by reformists; but black students have never on a large scale been success-ful at passing these tests. They too, like the "whole language" reading method, have backfired. Instead of ensuring equality by giving all students the exact same "objectified" test, they mediated a further widening of the academic gap between black and white students. The School is not going to be able to address over 200 years of learned behavior with a standardized test. However, the School can address the issue with a grassroots pedagogy of the masses.

In developing such a pedagogy we must account for the history of people of African descent in America; however, we must not be crippled by it. We must not define ourselves or others as victims. Not unlike most urban centers across the nation, the relationship of the School in Houston with African American parents in *The Bottoms* has been crippled by this history. Parents, living products of that history, have become victims and they have *learned* to be *powerless*; meaning they have abdicated their responsibility to a sense of hopelessness. The primary component of a pedagogy of the masses has to have a solid plan for engaging parents in dialogue, first with education and then with the School. Parents must come to appreciate education as something that is not only assigned to the domain of the School.

Freire says that there are two distinct stages in the pedagogy of the oppressed. The first stage must deal with the oppressed consciousness. It must deal with the problem of people who oppress and people who are oppressed. It must take into account their worldview, their behavior, and their morals. It must deal with how they have come to the place they are now; and that place must be defined. They must identify the causes of their oppression, not only the symptoms of it. They must make linked and informed decisions to transform the situation and create a new one. In the second stage, the reality of oppression has already been transformed, and then this pedagogy is no longer a pedagogy of the oppressed but one of the people in the process of permanent liberation–I call this transformation a pedagogy of the masses.

My friend who lived in Third Ward and who was desperately looking for a suitable middle school for her son got an idea that demonstrates this process. She used Freire's discourse as a basis for her master's thesis, which she called a "pedagogy of being."

She describes it as: "you—being who you are—as you are—essentially is in itself a pedagogy." In relation to how this concept would be applied to education, and more specifically in schools and classrooms, she offers: "In your way of being, you deliver curriculum uniquely as you—as your self—simply by being who you are, how you are." She also added that the pedagogy of being is one that takes form within the spirit of the individual before it manifests to actions. She said to me that she'd been thinking about how such a pedagogy might look in operation. She thought it might look like organizing a "spiritual PTO"–a parent teacher organization that focuses on addressing the issues of our schools through spiritual action.

I was intrigued. I offered to help her organize the idea and set it up as a national and international social networking platform that would create a globally unified effort to transform education from the dismal situation that exists today to one that is life-giving, hope-filled, creative, and inspiring. Imagine transforming our traditional educational system from one of bubbling in multiple choice circles, to one in which people like Mark Zuckerberg (Facebook creator), Steve Jobs (Apple creator), and Michael Jackson (who needs no description) can flourish. This is a perfect example of a pedagogy of the masses.

In the next Chapter, I give an overview of some of the other programs that I have designed and implemented over the past seven years and have found to be effective programs for transforming schools like the schools in *The Bottoms*.

THE EPILOGUE

Born of the Research

In some ways I have a conflict of interest in writing this book. *Conflict of Interest.* My interests are in conflict. I have a sincere interest in making sure that children are cared for and that they have access to structures that support their well-being. *Well-being.* Being is who we are. The "being" of us carries the DNA of our purpose, which holds the instructions of our intellectual personality, our spiritual acumen and the essence of our souls—being is the *essence* of who we are. I remember describing essence to my undergraduate students this way: The essence of a pen is that it writes. The essence of myself is that I build support structures for children that ensure their beings (the essence of their selves) are well.

Recently, I discovered that my passion for protecting children and making sure they are whole in every aspect of their lives comes from my own childhood experiences with poverty. My father died when I was five years old. Before that, we were poor, but we had stability. My parents owned the land that we lived on. My father worked very, very hard to ensure we had all of what we needed and some of what we wanted. He gave me a sense of constancy and steadiness. My mother was very industrious. While my father worked, she built our first house (literally built with hammer and nails and 2x4s). She had an impeccable conviction of the idea of possibilities. My mother gave me "dreams." She also gave me hope, intellectual curiosity, the belief that I could do anything I wanted, and an intimate connection to the Divine. Nevertheless, when my father died, so did my family's sense of stability, which we traded (inadvertently, but naturally) for my mother's own childhood experiences with the instability of poverty (when she was thirteen years old, circumstances forced her to live on the streets). We fell into a deep, deep "space of poverty."

A space of poverty reflects not only the physical structures of poverty like one's house: Our house was the raggediest (not sure that's really a word) house on the block. On the day that I graduated from high school, it rained. It was a long rain, but not necessarily a hard rain. There was no storm. Nevertheless, when we came home from the ceremony, the ceiling in my bedroom had collapsed from the rain, ruining all of my high school memorabilia. I and my mother and my sisters noticed that I cried way too hard about the loss of these things. The loss of pep rally souvenirs and my signature book, in which my classmates and teachers had written the same nice words that they had written in everybody else's signature book. I cried like someone had died. It broke my heart. Thus, a space of poverty also reflects your self-confidence, your worldview, your dreams...and your heart.

It took me many years to realize (I love that word *real-ize*–to make real) why I was so devastated by the loss of such seemingly valueless trinkets. Coming home to see the ceiling lying on my bed was like watching my heart cave in. I had never understood the existence of poverty. The caved-in ceiling looked exactly like how my heart felt after years of soaking disappointments. There were times when I went to sleep so that I would not know how hungry I was. There were times when I watched my mother (a very strong woman, not only physically strong, but also emotionally and mentally) break from the strain of placing too much hope in dreams that ended with sleep. Forty-four years after my father's death, I broke the convincing hold that poverty had on my life. Unfortunately, however, before I broke it, I passed it on to my daughter.

The lack of stability manifested itself in my daughter's life very differently from how it did in mine. In my life, it presented itself as a financial deficiency. When I was twenty-one, my mother sold our house to her pastor because she needed the money. She had tried to get my sisters to keep it in the family because she knew the land would be very valuable some day. They were so damaged by the poverty of their experience in that place that they couldn't see it. I was terribly depressed, married in a bad relationship, pregnant, and broke. So we lost the house. Furthermore, I felt a deep sense of betrayal. The buyer, who was my mother's pastor at that time, had taken so much from my mother over forty years: Time, energy, emotion, care (when his first wife was dying with cancer, my mother cared for her around the clock until she died, at no charge); but he had never really been present for her when she needed him, except to *buy* her house. He only paid her $5000 for it. That broke my heart.

That feeling of "not valuable" crept into my self-esteem. The history that led my mother to so undervalue her property was the same history that led me to develop defenses to protect my self-esteem from the same such undervaluing. To overcompensate for what I really thought about my worth to the world, I presented an extremely high self-confidence. People who didn't know me well thought I was arrogant, which I could not understand.

My mother's affection for marginalized people, had firmly established a similar affection in me as well—never mind the fact that I saw myself as a marginalized person. I was always drawn to people who nobody wanted to be around. I befriended people that nobody wanted to befriend. But in business, if I felt threatened, I would rely on my intelligence and knowledge and talk over the head of my opposition in an attempt to make them feel small and uninformed. I used my intelligence as a weapon. And since most people only knew me in business, because I kept my private life very secluded, they said I was arrogant. One morning, while sitting on the ground of my childhood home, I *realized* (Again: I love that word: real-*ized*–made real) that the reason I had been so offended by a recent job interaction was because, despite the fact that I had done everything "they" said I should do, it was still not good enough.

A Confession

So here's what happened: After my daughter's death, I had been out of work for a year and a half. I was so depressed that I had no energy to do anything but sleep. So a year and a half of not working, left me needing work badly. My pastor, and my friend, Rudy, encouraged me to apply for work with a national charter school organization. Rudy knows the co-founder and agreed to introduce me. I hesitantly agreed. I was hesitant because I didn't want what I call a *job* job. I used to think my inability to work a traditional job was a flaw, but later came to understand that it was a gift–I build things from scratch and build systems around it for other people to manage. When I reached out to Rudy's contact, he referred me to his recruiter. I sent my CV to the recruiter, who responded immediately with excitement about my expertise and experience in education: A PhD, eighteen years in public education, co-founding a public middle school in NYC, consulting with government leaders in South Africa, Malawi, Cuba and Mexico. He said he would talk to his leadership team and get back to me. A week later, the recruiter sent me an email asking me if I would be interested in a K-12 classroom teaching position. I was taken aback. I know the experience of their teachers and they don't have my background. Most of their leaders don't have my background. I was confused. After pondering the question for two days, I responded with one word: No. He said, after speaking with his leadership team, the only thing he could offer me was a link to apply for a teaching job.

I spent a couple of months trying to know why that offended me so much. Was I offended because I thought a K-12 teacher's position was beneath me? After some heavy soul searching, I realized no, I do not think teaching is beneath me. I love teaching and I believe it is one of the most honorable and valuable callings one can receive. I was offended by the organization that offered me the position...well, actually they just offered a link to apply to the position.

This organization is run by individuals who come from a tradition that has always identified me as an "outsider." And I was offended because once again, despite the fact that I had attended and done well at an ivy league university as an undergraduate, earned my master's and doctorate degrees at a world-renowned and respected university in New York City, traveled and worked around the world in education policy with government leaders, started a middle school, taught grades seven through university and mentored new teachers, the only job that this organization's leadership team thought I was qualified to apply for in their organization was a teacher's job. Upon having this realization, I also realized that it was this type of devaluing of my self that had caused me to build defense walls around myself that looked like arrogance. I had decided: Not only am I good enough to play with you, in fact, I am better than you. But it was just a defense. And I only employed it when I felt threatened. It had been useful to me, for a time. However, had I not experienced this encounter I would not have been freed from this bondage because I didn't know it was there. This experience revealed it, so I could deal with. At the end of that encounter, that defense mechanism was no longer needed.

While processing this event, I also still needed to work badly. I was running out of money. I felt drawn to enroll in a financial freedom class held at my church. It's a ten-week class. That's what they tell me. I could have sworn it was twelve weeks. It was a loooong class. But I could tell it was so important for me to go that I was afraid not to go. I had said to the facilitator: "I don't think this class is for me. It seems too basic." But he felt strongly that I should attend. So I did. Six months after completing the class, it was revealed why it had been important for me to sit in that class, learning nothing new to help my financial situation. I understood that everything we see and don't see, and everything we do and don't do is created and managed in the spirit realm. Poverty had an intense and convincing hold on my life and had been spiritually created on the grounds of my childhood home and managed for decades in my life. It did not matter what knowledge, degrees, jobs, and connections I had, I could not escape poverty.

So I needed to sit in that class for ten weeks in order for there to be a spiritual excavation process of digging up old seeds of poverty and planting new seeds of wealth. You see, these spiritual ways of being in our lives are established or excavated through a process. The spiritual change is instantaneous. But the physical reflection is procedural. Sitting in the class had excavated those poverty seeds, and while sitting on the ground where those seeds had been born, I buried them and left them there. Two weeks after I buried those seeds of poverty, my company got a large one-year contract that has been renewed each year afterwards.

The spiritual condition of instability manifested itself in my daughter's life through a restlessness that left her feeling unsettled and not fully loved. When Milah (my daughter) was born, there was no one at the hospital with us but the hospital staff. Unlike when her older brother was born—all my family was there to greet him as he entered the world. The birthing of my daughter was a very depressing moment for me. (Ironically I was not present for her, when she gave birth to her children). My mother was taking a class. I was estranged from most of my sisters. My husband at that time was hiding from the hospital. We thought if the hospital knew I had a husband they'd attempt to bill me for the service of delivering the baby; so when I went into labor, he dropped me off at the entrance to the emergency room (these are legacies of poverty).

When Milah made her entrance into this big old world, the doctor laid her in my arms, but I was so exhausted from the eight hours of labor and seventeen years of the kind of emotional pain that comes from being poor in the richest nation in the world and that produces the kind of mental exhaustion that begs you to sleep unnaturally, that I asked the nurse to please take her because I was afraid I might drop her.

When Milah and her brother were toddlers, their father and I took them to stay with his parents in Detroit for the summer. It was a horrible mistake. We left them while they slept. Milah never got over the feeling of abandonment; and yet she passed on the same practice to her two children. She regularly left them with family members to go to parties, to travel or just because. Her children rarely slept in their own beds. Two and half years ago, Milah was murdered. On July 12, 2010 I got a phone call from my son. He said: "Mama, I think Milah's been killed." I fell to my knees in a wail that was so loud and so hard I actually didn't recognize it as me. At about 3:00 or 4:00 the next morning, while I was in a cry so deep that the only thing

I could hear was my own tears, God said from the center of my spirit: "She's with me." The only way I could have heard God was that it had to have come from a place deeper than my cry. A *center* place. A place of *centering*. That *centering experience* would prove to be my saving grace over the next two years. However, at that moment all I could think was: God, how could you let that happen? I fell into a deep darkness, and I sat there for a year and half.

In that period of silence, I had time to reflect on how the legacy of instability engendered by the historical poverty entrenched in our family had impacted us. Fortunately, before Milah transitioned we had a chance to tell each other all the things you might want to say to someone before they die (it was providential). After her death, I tried to bring her children to live with me to offer them an opportunity to experience stability, but the family of Milah's father (my first ex-husband) saw that gesture as an indictment on their lifestyle; so, they fought it. The children's father sided with them. So the children are living in Detroit, and they still rarely sleep in their own beds.

This history of African peoples in this nation is wrought with layers upon layers of complexity. We pass on these complex layers in strange ways, most of which we are not even aware. But we must do better.

When I was a little girl, I said I would never have children or get married. But, I was born and raised in a time and place where getting married and having children is what little girls grew up to do. So I did get married and had two kids. That's why I began this chapter by talking about my *conflict of interest*. My interests are in conflict. I have a sincere interest in making sure that children are cared for, but I had an inability to connect intimately with my own children when they were younger (a consequence of my own history as a child). Nevertheless, also because of my own arduous childhood, I connect with the *cries* of children for equality, justice, economic stability and access to quality education. I have a passion for making sure children are holistically whole.

So I have developed several programs that create structures that allow our educational system to connect with the intimate needs of our children; and I pray that someday my own grandchildren will benefit from these programs, since today I cannot give to them directly.

Programs

The first program I created was a **tutoring program**. One of our first students was a fifth grader who had not passed the state exam and had been retained in fifth grade for two years before we worked with her. We discovered that the student was distressed by reading silently. This information was reported to her principal, who arranged for the student to use a device that is linked from the mouth to the ear, allowing the student to read quietly into it and hear it in a normal tone in the ear. The student not only, for the first time, completed the exam, but she passed it! In a large classroom, this fifth grader, who acted out when instructed to read silently, had been considered to be a "behavioral problem." In contrast, in the small-setting environment that we created, we were able to understand why she was not making progress.

We offer individual attention to each child's data, learning gaps, weaknesses, strengths, and learning styles. Eighty-five percent of our students passed the Texas state standardized exam in our first year. Eighty-two percent passed in our second year. Some of those students had been retained for one or two years before coming to our program. After working with them for four months, they achieved success.

Another program that I designed is a social media project intended to help students at risk of dropping out of school to stay in school. We call it **#doSchool**. The hash tag in the title speaks to the way that communities are developed in today's world of technology. The # symbol is used on Twitter to categorize ideas and therefore create a community of followers around those ideas. #doSchool's mission is to meet young people where they are, and use the tools that they are already using, to help them do what they need to do–help them *do school*. The program uses reality documentary, social networking, an academic advisor, and the students themselves to create twenty-first century iCommunities designed to intervene in the dropout process and provide real time support through social media technology.

We implemented the program as a pilot in January 2012. Twenty-five students began the program. Within the first week, we matriculated half the students out of the program by enrolling them into the correct academic program. We discovered that at least half of the students at risk of not completing school are at risk because they are not in the correct academic program. Half of our students were eighteen years old or older and had less than five of the twenty-two credits required to graduate. We helped these students enroll into GED programs that allow them to transition smoothly into community college and/or certification training.

Half of the remaining students were required by their school to enroll into a program where in they were able to make up lost attendance credits. The percentage of students who matriculated in #doSchool significantly out-paced the GED and attendance recapture programs that were required by the school. Each one of our students reported that #doSchool was a primary influence on them staying in school. Three of those students were nearly lost; however because of the personal attention, the individual relationship we developed with each student, and the customized plan we developed for each student we were able to keep those students in school.

We piloted the program as an after-school class. However, launching it as a school-wide program that is available during the school day as part of the class calendar is highly recommended. Most of the students who are at risk of dropping out of school do not make it past lunch. They leave the campus. Therefore it is unreasonable to expect students to stay for a longer day and to come to an afterschool program. As well, many of these students have adult responsibilities after school, which are often the reason they are dropping out of school. Running this program during the school day and on a more wide-scale basis will benefit the school tremendously.

Launching #doSchool was a significant challenge because of the lack of **technological infrastructure** found in schools with underserved populations. In my eighteen years of work in public education with marginalized populations, I have come to understand that one of the biggest challenges for advancing excellence for these students is the technological infrastructure and quality of data in the schools they attend. We teamed up with a local university to address this challenge with a local school district in Houston.

Through a partnership with a university, we built out the technological infrastructure of a local school district with a systems overhaul of the district's technological compatibility, connectivity, modularity, and IT personnel with the fundamental purpose of making it possible for the district to identify and monitor students that are at risk of leaving school prematurely, and to follow the progress of the entire student population. At the time of this partnership, this district's graduation rate was at thirty-seven and a half percent. The district is a medium size district and does not have the capacity internally to develop its technological production of data that can be used to identify students early who are at-risk of dropping out of school or monitoring the progress of students. This type of partnership allows a university to share their resources with a struggling school district to reach a goal that they are unable to reach alone. I would like to see this project established nationally to advance educational excellence. It would provide technological resources to build districts' capabilities to identify students early, place them in appropriate intervention programs and monitor progress.

Another very serious deficiency in schools with marginalized populations is the teaching staff. It is nationally recognized that one of the most critical components to improving student achievement is having an effective teaching staff. Teacher quality accounts for seven point five percent of variation in student achievement—by far the largest single factor and about the same amount as a grade level (Rivkin, Hanushek, & Kain, 1999).

At the beginning of the 2011-2012 school year, forty teachers of a Houston school district (about eight percent) had a student roster with less than half of their students passing the most recent State exams. The Superintendent charged me with developing a process for supporting these teachers with a systemic practice that would support professional achievement for teachers as a critical foundation to supporting improved student achievement. We determined that an effective model to work with this cohort of teachers would be a model of "embedded professional development" with a professional development coach, known as a **Professional Achievement Coach**. The Coach is an on-site professional developer who coaches educators in proven instructional methods. Instructional coaching is grounded in current research and clinical knowledge on leadership and schools as "professional communities of practice." I designed the program's infrastructure, which consists of the goals, procedures, the systemic tools to be used for carrying out the program, and the philosophy of the program, which offered a promising new professional development practice in which teacher

leaders serve as coaches to facilitate and guide professional learning for a school's teachers.

In keeping with the notion of teacher development, I
also implemented **Post-Graduate Content Seminars**
on the high school campus of a Houston school district
to support math and science teachers with content
knowledge that enhances students' understanding of
natural phenomena and develops students' math and
science process skills. Many of the teachers teaching
math and science in low performing urban schools of
color do not know their content. In my experience, more
than half of the "math" teachers of low performing
urban public schools do not know math, and likewise,
more than half of the "science" teachers do not know
science. To most people who don't spend as much time
in these schools as I do, this is a shocking revelation.
But it is such a common occurrence in the schools that I
work in, that it has unfortunately become familiar to
me. As I pointed out earlier, the Education Trust reports
that more than two-thirds of fifth to eighth grade
students receive math instruction from teachers who do
not have a degree or certificate in math. In addition,
ninety-three percent of students in those grades are
taught physical sciences by teachers with no degree or

certificate in physical sciences. Furthermore, in high poverty schools, students are assigned teachers who lack the qualification to teach mathematics at twice the rate of white students.

My goal in designing the Post-Graduate Content Seminars for the Houston school was to offer teachers a university level experience that would entice teachers to attend, because although their campus had less than forty percent of their students graduating, school administrators could not force teachers to attend these classes. One of the tragedies of public education is how the system is set up to protect the rights of adults at the expense of children. The Superintendent of this district had been visited a couple of times by the local teacher's union because of complaints that teachers had filed as a result of programs the Superintendent and I had introduced to bolster student achievement. It was a shameful experience. So I designed the class to mimic a university class, hoping teachers would recognize the opportunity as a privilege and see the benefit to enhancing their knowledge. Therefore, for attending the class (which was held on their campus to make it as convenient as possible) teachers received continuing educational program credits; the courses were taught by

PhD experts in the content and in education; and the course was a six-week course, delivered once per week for two hours.

The math seminar assisted teachers in improving their mathematics instruction, by focusing on how to implement techniques designed to improve learning among diverse groups of learners that lead to increased mathematics achievement and proficiency. Each workshop had mathematics content as the context and focused on mathematical practices. The facilitator also prepared teachers for the math content exam. Of the ten "math" teachers on that campus, three of them (thirty percent) had not passed the math content exam to be a math teacher.

The science facilitator delivered workshops that covered science content, as well as science delivery models. Participants learned how to implement the 5E Instructional Model, which supports students in building their own understanding of new ideas through the 5E process: Engage, Explore, Explain, Extend and Evaluate. The facilitator also planned units with participants, modeled lessons for participants, and supported participants in preparing for the science content exam. The school only had two full-time "science" teachers on staff, the rest of the teachers who taught science were substitutes who did not have a science certification or a degree in science. Of the two full-time "science" teachers, one of those had repeatedly taken the science certification exam, but failed to pass it.

Experiences like those described here led me to form an anthropological education firm, Anthropologi Educational Research and Development. I had no intention of actually starting a business. However, the success of our tutors began to spread throughout Houston. Principals outside of *The Bottoms* began asking me for tutors. One day, I was sitting in a principal's office and I explained that the program worked in conjunction with a class at University of Houston, and therefore the number of available tutors depended on how many university students signed up for the class. But, I said if you can afford to pay for tutors, then I can get you as many as you want. She signed up for three tutors. I had similar meetings with three other principals. That year, we placed twenty tutors in schools across Houston. In that moment, my firm was born.

I named this educational development firm Anthropologi—replacing the last letter of the word with "i" instead of "y" to emphasize the significance of the individual in the process of fixing broken schools. The study of anthropology is the study of human behavior in distinct cultural settings. At its core, it is about human diversity and seeks to facilitate understanding between groups of people by translating each group's culture to the other. Therefore anthropology is the perfect tool to use to understand why so many of our nation's children fail school, while other students do well. It is through anthropology that I have been able to understand the pedagogy of distressed urban public schools, as well as to explore my own personal journey in the grassroots pedagogy of the masses.

This pedagogy is what my journey in public education has been about. As someone who grew up in an area that was oppressed by poverty and in a family situation that lacked the stability that a child needs to thrive, I overcame that situation, looked back and created platforms to bring about change. I experienced what it is to *be*...in the face of *becoming*....

ABOUT THE AUTHOR

Dr. Sharon Washington is an education anthropologist and the founder of Anthropologi Educational Research and Development, an international firm created to bring "education" back to schools. She is also the creator and host of *Education Made Visible*, an education news talk show designed to bring the public back into public schools, and to take the conversation of education beyond the bureaucracy of schools. For the past eighteen years, Dr. Washington's work has taken place on the frontlines of urban education in some of the most dilapidated communities in the United States. In these communities, she has designed and implemented several programs that have helped to create more purposeful learning environments for K-12 students. This book, her first, is the result of that work.

Dr. Washington has also worked in education research, policy analysis, program design, and teacher preparation in various parts of the world. That work includes school design, teacher certification, and leadership development in the United States; policy work in South Africa; research on the role of autonomous schools in the technology of a revolution in Chiapas, Mexico; the politics of education in Cuba; and the definition of school and its role in economic development in Malawi. Sharon has lectured at New School University and the University of Houston; and taught students in grades 6-12.

She has worked as a journalist for six years. Her writings have appeared in the Dallas Times Herald, the Akron Beacon Journal, and New York Newsday.

Dr. Washington has a PhD and a master's degree in anthropology from The New School for Social Research in New York City. She received her undergraduate degree from Columbia University in New York City, where she graduated with a major in cinema and media theory. She studied the role of cinema and media images on "Third World" imaginations. Sharon lives in Houston, TX with her son, Dennis and his wife Tristan.

20196234R00140